Forecasting Terrorism

Indicators and Proven Analytic Techniques

Sundri Khalsa

With the assistance of Martin Gordon,
Consulting Editor

The Scarecrow Press, Inc.
Lanham, Maryland • Toronto • Oxford
2004

SCARECROW PRESS, INC.

Published in the United States of America
by Scarecrow Press, Inc.
A wholly owned subsidiary of
The Rowman & Littlefield Publishing Group, Inc.
4501 Forbes Boulevard, Suite 200, Lanham, Maryland 20706
www.scarecrowpress.com

PO Box 317
Oxford
OX2 9RU, UK

The author is donating the royalties from this book to the nonprofit National Memorial Institute for the Prevention of Terrorism (www.mipt.org) and the Joint Military Intelligence College Foundation, which supports the Defense Intelligence Agency, Joint Military Intelligence College (www.dia.mil/Jmic/).

The views expressed in this work are those of the author and do not reflect the official policy or position of the Department of Defense or the United States Government. This work has been approved for unrestricted public release by the Office of the Secretary of Defense (Public Affairs). The case number for this approval is 02-S-2656, issued by the Department of Defense Directorate for Freedom of Information and Security Review.

British Library Cataloguing in Publication Information Available

Library of Congress Cataloging-in-Publication Data

Khalsa, Sundri, 1975–
  Forecasting terrorism : indicators and proven analytic techniques / Sundri Khalsa.
    p. cm.
  Includes bibliographical references and index.
  ISBN 0-8108-5017-6 (pbk. : alk. paper)
  1. Terrorism—Forecasting. 2. Terrorism—Prevention. I. Title.

HV6431.K426 2004
363.32'01'12—dc22

2004015785

♾™ The paper used in this publication meets the minimum requirements of American National Standard for Information Sciences—Permanence of Paper for Printed Library Materials, ANSI/NISO Z39.48-1992.
Manufactured in the United States of America.

For all those who have lost life, loved ones, and liberty due to terrorism.
For all those who have worked to protect against terrorism.

Contents

Figures

Figures

Tables

Preface

The unit chief of the Federal Bureau of Investigation (FBI) Counterterrorism Division Threat Monitoring Unit characterized this forecasting methodology as "light-years ahead." Officials in the Defense Intelligence Agency (DIA) identified this system as "the bedrock for the evolving approach to terrorism analysis" and an "unprecedented forecasting model." FBI and CIA officials invited me to implement this terrorism forecasting system at FBI Headquarters in September 2002. In addition, FBI Threat Monitoring Unit officials arranged multiple briefings for the CIA, the United States interagency Foreign Terrorist Tracking Task Force, and National Security Council staff at the White House Executive Office Building. Response has been highly enthusiastic and supportive, but the funding, time, and people necessary to implement the system (about $250,000, 6 months, and 107 people) have been roadblocks to full implementation.

My goal in publishing this book is to gain the attention of those who have the authority to implement this system and for the royalties from this book to be used to further support counterterrorism efforts. All of the royalties from this book are being donated to the nonprofit National Memorial Institute for the Prevention of Terrorism (www.mipt.org) and the Joint Military Intelligence College Foundation, which supports the Defense Intelligence Agency, Joint Military Intelligence College (www.dia.mil/Jmic/). Additionally, this book makes the methodology available for free to those organizations that work to help prevent terrorism.

The views expressed in this work do not reflect the official policy or position of the Department of Defense (DoD) or the U.S. Government. This work has been approved for unrestricted public release by the Office of the Secretary of Defense (Public Affairs). The case number for this approval is 02-S-2656, which was issued by the DoD Directorate for Freedom of Information and Security Review (DFOISR).

Some of the best improvements to this methodology have developed out of people's questions and criticisms. Please do not hesitate to contact me if you have input. You can reach me at SundriKK@hotmail.com. Thank you for your attention because counterterrorism analysis efforts can make a difference in saving lives.

Acknowledgments

The Joint Military Intelligence College (JMIC) at the Defense Intelligence Agency (DIA) provided the forum for this research and work. JMIC supports and encourages research on intelligence issues that distills lessons and improves support to policy-level and operational consumers.

With special thanks to: My mother, Gurumeet Kaur Khalsa, for comprehensive and detailed editing, for graphics consulting, for helping to present complex ideas clearly and resolve complex concepts, and for inspiring key ideas. Maj Robert Whitaker, USAF, for causing the transformation of this research and complex ideas from a near incompressible text to a clear and understandable presentation, for challenging and inspiring key ideas, for providing a reality check, and for going above and beyond. CDR Steven Carey, USN, for helping to resolve complex concepts and present complex ideas clearly, as well as for inspiring key ideas. Special Agent Steve Hooper, FBI, for taking time to listen to new ideas and pushing them up the chain and for invaluable feedback. Col Octavio Biaz, USAF, for supporting, challenging, and inspiring improvement in these ideas as they were first developing at the Air Force Office of Special Investigations, 24th Expeditionary Field Investigations Squadron, in Riyadh, Saudi Arabia, August 2000 to August 2001. Those who inspired and supported key ideas as they were developing in Riyadh, Saudi Arabia: Special Agent Doyle Riggan, USAF; MSgt Mark Cannon, USAF; Special Agent Alex Gutierrez, USAF; MSgt Danny Garcia, USAF; CMSgt Arthur Payton, USAF; and Special Agent John Ryan, DEA. Those who clarified intelligence collectors' needs and provided guidance on how to improve analysts' communication with collectors: Mr. Tom Fields; Special Agent Barry Fisher, USAF; Mr. Bill Halpin; Mr. James Dixon; and Mr. Donald Day. Capt Jacqueline Chang, USAF, for her persistent encouragement to present these ideas to the FBI, inspiring key concepts, and helping to convey complex ideas clearly. Capt Naomi Stankow-Mercer, USA, for helping to resolve complex concepts and convey complex ideas clearly. Special Agent Art Cummings, FBI, for pushing to get this system implemented at the FBI. Those who provided invaluable technical assistance: David Morse; SSgt Felicia O'Neal, USAF; Kenji Hayashi; MSgt Kevin Selwyn, USAF; Ray Gomez; Ronnie Foxe; and Sean Nieburg. Those who gave invaluable feedback and/or support: Capt Alan Todl, USMC; Ann Sarkes, FBI; Anthony Bargar; CDR Beckey Lewis, USN; Betty O'Hearn; Charles Hoing; Charlie Clopper; Cindy Blackstone, FBI; Dan Gressang; Capt Darla Gardner, USAF; Mr. David Hungerford; Debbie Moody; Eric Matthews; Capt Eric Troil, USAF; Ambassador Francis Taylor; Garey Greco; Special Agent Heather Robacker, USAF; Jed Kukowski, FBI; Jennifer Lahei, FBI; Jim Major; Capt Jim Wacker, USAF; Special Agent John Robertson, FBI; LCDR Jorge Gracia, USN; Kim Hawk, FBI; Special Agent Lionel Baren, FBI; Matthew Devost; Lt Col Max Blood, USAF; Martin Gordon; Melissa Ray; Nicole Carty; SSgt Noland, USAF; Col Ray Bradley, USAF; Roger Krondin, FBI; Capt Russ Powell, USAF; Dr. Russ Swenson; Sandra Seal, FBI; Col Scott Deacon, USAF; Scott Parker; CAPT Steve Richarson, USN; Special Agent Steve Roehrick, USAF; Sue Eason; CAPT Tom Facer, USN; Special Agent Tom Gilkison, USAF; and Gen Victor Renuart, USAF.

Those who have been a caring and inspirational part of my life: My father, Eric Fimbres; Alex Mouw; Ally; Alma Moritz; Amarjit; Amrit Mantar; Amy Pickerell; Andrew Ledford; Angela Agne; Ann Conely; Annet Smith; April Moore; CMSgt Arthur Payton, USAF; B. J. Fry; Barnee Rigg; Barry Stout; Betty Hopperstad; Bhagwan; Bibiji; Bill McGoey; Bobby Farina; Brandon Fewer; Brian Conn; Brian O'Connell; Bryan McManus; Chandra Kirin; Chris Cederholm; Chris Duffley; Christiana Thompson; Christine Fimbres; Conrad Fimbres; Crystal Konopka; Cynthia Agra; David Kramer; Debbie Wee; Dev Amrit; Dharam Kaur; Dharam Singh; Donna Sikora; Cpl Dustin Smith, USMC; Ed Yealdhall; E. J. Enju; Eldon Metzger; Eric Egland; Eric Leuenberger; Ethan Rigg; Evan Smith; Gar Lightner; Georgie Faine; Georgia Parworth-King; CAPT Gerald Stoll,USN; Greg Harmon; Gina Richter; Guru Amrit; Guru Dev; Guru Ditta; Guru Jaswant; Guru Kirn S.; Guru Tej; Hanz Staffelbach; Hari Jot; Heidi Merrell-Gurnwald; Himat Khalsa; Irma; Lt Col James Gallowy III, USAF; Jamie Stephens; Jayne Apo; Jennifer Auchter-Herrington; Jenny Fimbres; Jesse Elizarde; Jill; Jim Steen; Joe Fimbers; John Burns; John Carroll; John Goodhue; John Silance; John Sporer; Jorge Borunda; Kalai; Kamille; Karan Kharan; Karen Chandler; Kathy Badgley; Kerry Schreider; Capt Kirk Kimmett, USAF; Kirsten Sanders; Kirtan Khalsa; Laura; Leisa Birch; Lia Reynolds; Major Lewis Carlisle, USAF; Loan McIntosh-Rupp; Louis McCray; Madhur Nain; Mahan Kirn; Maiko Nemoto; Manjit; Margaret DiLaura; Mari Fries; Marie Conway; Mark Connell; Mark Everson; Mark Haseman; SSgt Mark Murray, USAF; Mark Wood; Mary Fimbres; Mary-Beth Larson; Melissa Monette; Michelle Johnson; Mike Gavornic; Mike Grunwald; Mike Rhodes; Molly Cunningham; Nadine; Natasha Zigler; Amn Nicole Ryan, USAF; Nikki Cushman; Norm Prue; Paul Kim; Pritham B.; Pritham; Rachael; Reina Schoorl; Capt Richard Glenn, USAF; Russ Holland; Ryan McFadden; Sam Scafe; Sara LaFone; Sat Batchan; Sat Hari; Sat Jeet; Sat Kirin; Sat Simran; Sat Sunderta; CPT Scott Koast, USA; Scott McPeak; Siri Sat; Siri Simran Sr.; Siri Simran; Siri Singh Sahib; Siri Sunderi; Stephanie Menard; Stephanie Wyatt; Steve Marker; Tamara Mason; Terrence Joyce; Tim Fetsch; Tim Teal; Tom Cox; Capt Tom Duong, USAF; Tom Miner; Tony Weis; Veronique Dillon; Vick Lomupo; Vicky Ledden; Yvonne Houchen; and many more.

Introduction

Surprise occurs not in the absence of enemy awareness, but in spite of it.
Major Jeffery O'Leary, USAF, "Surprise and Intelligence: Towards a Clearer Understanding." *Air Power Journal*, (Spring 1994).

The enclosed compact disc (CD) has the website interface to a methodology to forecast terrorist attacks. The CD also has a 45-minute video that provides an executive summary of the forecasting methodology. It would be helpful for the reader to watch the video before reading the book. The CD should automatically open to the web homepage (otherwise click on the file called "index" to open the web homepage). The video is accessible from the web homepage via the hyperlink "Forecasting Methodology."

This book provides: a step-by-step explanation of how to forecast terrorism (chapter 1), an evaluation of the forecasting system against the 42 common warning pitfalls that have caused warning failures in the past (chapter 2), and recommendations for implementation (chapter 3). This forecasting methodology uses proven analytical techniques and guards against 82 percent of the 42 common warning pitfalls that experts have identified throughout history. Three key lessons stand out from the study of warning failures. The Intelligence Community's current approach to terrorism warning does not reflect an understanding of these 3 lessons. The methodology proposed here offers the Intelligence Community a solution that incorporates these lessons.

Lesson 1: Analysis, Rather Than Collection, Is the Most Effective Way to Improve Warning

Although improvements in collection are needed, these improvements do not address the predominant problems in intelligence warning. Warning failures are rarely due to inadequate intelligence collection, are more frequently due to weak analysis, and are most often due to decision makers ignoring intelligence.[1] Decision makers, however, ignore intelligence when analysis is weak.[2] Thus, the problem again points to analysis.

Rather than analysis, the focus to improve warning normally turns to collection.[3] That trend continues after September 11, 2001, with the Intelligence Community's consensus that terrorism warning improvement can best be achieved through collection, rather than analysis.[4]

Empirical research, however, shows that more information does *not* improve the *accuracy* of analysts' assessments; it merely improves analysts' *certainty* in their assessments.[5] Additional research even finds, "an intensified collection effort does not necessarily lead to better analysis and more accurate estimates; when the additional information contains a large portion of noise, the risks of another intelligence failure leading to surprise may even increase."[6] Furthermore, "it is sometimes assumed that counterterrorism analysis suffers from a dearth of intelligence. Actually the opposite is the problem—there is too much intelligence. . . . As with all intelligence analysts, value-added analysis requires an ability to separate out . . . the signals from the noise."[7] The evidence suggests there is more value in the available information than current analytical technique reveals.

Lesson 2: Hiring Smart People Does Not Necessarily Lead to Good Analysis

Many argue that "the best way to ensure high-quality analysis is to bring high quality analysts into the process."[8] Their reasoning is that many intelligent minds working together are bound to produce a good assessment. They're wrong, according to researchers.[9] Studies show that, "frequently groups of smart, well-motivated people . . . agree . . . on the wrong solution. . . . They didn't fail because they were stupid. They failed because *they followed a poor process in arriving at their decisions.*"[10]

Lesson 3: Systematic Process Is the Most Effective Way to Facilitate Good Analysis

There is a long-standing debate within the Intelligence Community over whether structured techniques work on complex problems, such as terrorism analysis.[11] The nonstructured approach has become the norm in the Intelligence Community.[12] Many analysts argue that structured techniques cannot account for the infinite number of variables involved in complex problems and that intuition can do better. However, research shows that intuitive judgments "seldom take proper account of all the information available."[13] People selectively remember information based on the vividness and recency of their exposure to it. "People have difficulty keeping more than seven or so 'chunks' of information in mind at once."[14] Psychological studies show that people tend to ignore evidence that does not support their biases and interpret ambiguous information as confirming their biases. When the mind is overwhelmed with information, that tendency is magnified as part of a simplification technique to reduce the information down to a manageable size.[15] Furthermore, "intuitive judgments suffer from serious random inconsistencies due to fatigue, boredom, and all the factors that make us human."[16] Many people argue that they can avoid these pitfalls by simply being aware of them, but empirical research shows that "tactics can improve your success beyond what you can achieve simply by being aware of the dangers."[17]

Many analysts think structured methods take too long.[18] If, however, an analyst makes data entry to the structured framework part of his daily routine, and even automates certain parts of the process for which he has made predetermined (intuitive) choices, then methodology can in fact save time rather than consume it.

Intuition cannot be eliminated from intelligence analysis because a great deal of intelligence information is *qualitative*—"information that can be captured that is not numerical in nature."[19] Since nonnumerical information cannot be counted, an analyst must assess its value subjectively using intuition.

A key misunderstanding in the debate over intuition versus structured technique is that an analyst must choose either intuition or structured technique.[20] In fact, both intuition and structured technique can be used together in a systematic process. "Anything that is qualitative can be assigned meaningful numerical values. These values can then be manipulated to help us achieve greater insight into the meaning of the data and to help us examine specific hypotheses."[21] It is not only possible to combine intuition and structure in a system; research shows the combination is more effective than intuition alone. "Considerable research suggests that you will maximize your chances of making the best choice if you find a systematic way to evaluate all the evidence favorable or unfavorable to each possible choice, compare the strength of evidence on each side rigorously, then pick the choice that your system indicates the evidence favors."[22] Thus, intelligence analysis must not only apply the art of intuition, but also the science of structured technique.

Finally, regardless of an analyst's individual opinion, decision makers have called on the Intelligence Community to use methodology.

> The Rumsfeld Commission noted that ". . . an expansion of the methodology used by the IC [Intelligence Community] is needed." . . . [Methodology] helps overcome mindset, keeps analysts who are immersed in a mountain of new information from raising the bar on what they would consider an alarming threat situation, and allows their minds to expand to other possibilities. Keeping chronologies, maintaining databases and arraying data are not fun or glamorous. These techniques are the heavy lifting of analysis, but this is what analysts are supposed to do. If decision makers only needed talking heads, those are readily available elsewhere.[23]

Since intuition cannot be eliminated from intelligence analysis, analysts must find a way to limit their vulnerability to the pitfalls of intuition. The methodology offered here combines the intuitive analytical technique with 4 structured analytical techniques—hypothesis testing, matrix logic, chronological sorting, and question set guidance.

The Merit of Current Analysis

There is an important point to make with due respect to terrorism analysts. "To say, 'The terrorist target set is an extremely difficult target set to work for a number of reasons,' truly understates the complexity of the problem."[24] Against that obstacle and limited resources, the counterterrorism community has devoted extensive efforts and achieved tremendous successes that are largely unnoticed.[25] In 1998 alone, some of those successes included but were not limited to: prevention of planned attacks against multiple targets in Montgomery, Alabama; St. Louis, Missouri; East St. Louis, Illinois; Los Angeles, California; Centralia, Illinois; and New York, New York, between February 23 and 26, 1998; prevention of a chemical attack in River Edge, New Jersey, April 8, 1998; prevention of a biological attack on government officials in McAllen Texas, July 1, 1998; and prevention of a bombing on an unspecified target, August 26, 1998.[26] The United States Counterterrorism Community's dedicated and talented professionals enabled those and many more successes.

Notes

1. Ronald D. Garst, "Fundamentals of Intelligence Analysis," in *Intelligence Analysis ANA 630*, no. 1, ed. Joint Military Intelligence College (Washington, D.C.: Joint Military Intelligence College, 2000): 7. Cited hereafter as Garst.

2. Hans Heymann Jr., "The Intelligence—Policy Relationship," in *Intelligence Analysis ANA 630*, no. 1 ed. Joint Military Intelligence College (Washington, D.C.: Joint Military Intelligence College, 2000): 55. Cited hereafter as Heymann.

3. Ephraim Kam, *Surprise Attack: The Victim's Perspective* (Cambridge, MA: Harvard University Press, 1988), 53. Cited hereafter as Kam.

4. A source, mid-level intelligence professional at a national intelligence organization, who wishes to remain anonymous, interview by author, 10 July 2002.

5. Garst, 23; Kam, 55.

6. Kam, 55.

7. Mark V. Kauppi, "Counterterrorism Analysis," *Defense Intelligence Journal* 11, no. 1, (Winter 2002): 39-53.

8. "Making Intelligence Smarter: The Future of U.S. Intelligence," *Report of an Independent Task Force* 1996, www.copi.com/articles/intelrpt/cfr.html (23 Jul. 1999).

9. J. Edward Russo and Paul J. H. Schoemaker, *Decision Traps: The Ten Barriers to Brilliant Decision-Making and How to Overcome Them* (New York: Rockefeller Center, 1989), 145. Cited hereafter as Russo.

10. Russo, 146. Additionally, the FBI's success with criminal profiling is an example of how applying a *systematic process* can produce an impressive record of accurate assessments. The profiling process has even enabled investigators to solve cases that had remained unsolved for many years. Ronald Kessler, *The FBI*, (New York: Pocket Books, 1993), 267.

11. Robert D. Folker, Jr., *Intelligence Analysis in Theater Joint Intelligence Centers: An Experiment in Applying Structured Methods*, Occasional Paper, no. 7 (Washington, D.C.: Joint Military Intelligence College, 2000), 7. Cited hereafter as Folker.

12. "A small number of analysts occasionally apply structured methods . . . but the traditional approach . . . is non-structured." Folker, 1.

13. Russo, 120.

14. Russo, 14.

15. Kam, 102, 106.

16. Russo, 135.

17. Russo, 115.

18. Folker, 7.

19. William M. K. Trochim, "Qualitative Data," *Cornell University: Research Methods Knowledge Base* 2002, http://trochim.human.cornell.edu/kb/qualdata.htm (31 May 2002).

20. Folker, 1.

21. William M. K. Trochim, "The Qualitative Debate," *Cornell University: Research Methods Knowledge Base* 2002, http://trochim.human.cornell.edu/kb/qualdeb.htm (31 May 2002).

22. Russo, 130.

23. Donald Rumsfeld, press conference, quoted in Mary O. McCarthy, "The Mission to Warn: Disaster Looms," *Defense Intelligence Journal* 7 no. 2 (Fall 1998): 21. Cited hereafter as McCarthy.

24. Major Robert L. Whitaker, USAF, Instructor, Joint Military Intelligence College, Washington, D.C., attachment to e-mail from Major Robert L. Whitaker, USAF, Instructor U.S. Joint Military Intelligence College, Washington, D.C. to author, 10 July 2002.

25. The author defines the Counterterrorism Community as: the various law enforcement agents, intelligence analysts and collectors, counterintelligence agents, scientific experts, emergency response personnel, and decision makers who are involved in combating terrorism.

26. Federal Bureau of Investigation (FBI), *Terrorism in the United States 1998* (Washington D.C.: FBI, 1998), 5-7; United States Department of State, *Patterns of Global Terrorism 1998* (Washington, D.C.: Office of the Secretary of State, 1999), 91.

Chapter 1

How to Forecast Terrorism:
Step-By-Step Explanation of the Methodology

Doing something systematic is better in almost all cases than seat-of-the-pants prediction.
    J. Edward Russo and Paul J. H. Schoemaker, *Decision Traps: The Ten Barriers to Brilliant Decision-Making and How to Overcome Them*

The Compact Disc (CD)

The forecasting assessments of this methodology are maintained on a website display. While reading the explanation of this methodology, it would be helpful for the reader to follow along on the webpage templates provided on the enclosed compact disc (CD). The CD should automatically open to the web homepage, which is shown at the top of figure 1.1 (otherwise click on the file called "index" to open the web homepage). Optimal viewing of the webpages requires a screen setting of 1024 by 768 pixels and the Microsoft Internet Explorer web browser.

The CD also includes a 45-minute video that provides an abbreviated step-by-step description of the methodology using the website display. The video is accessible from the web homepage via the hyperlink "Forecasting Methodology."

Overview of Methodology

The explanation of this methodology is going to begin at the lowest level of *indicators* and then build up to the big picture of countries within a region. Figure 1.1 shows a breakdown of the 3 primary types of warning picture views from the web homepage: 1) country list view, 2) target list view, and 3) indicator list view.

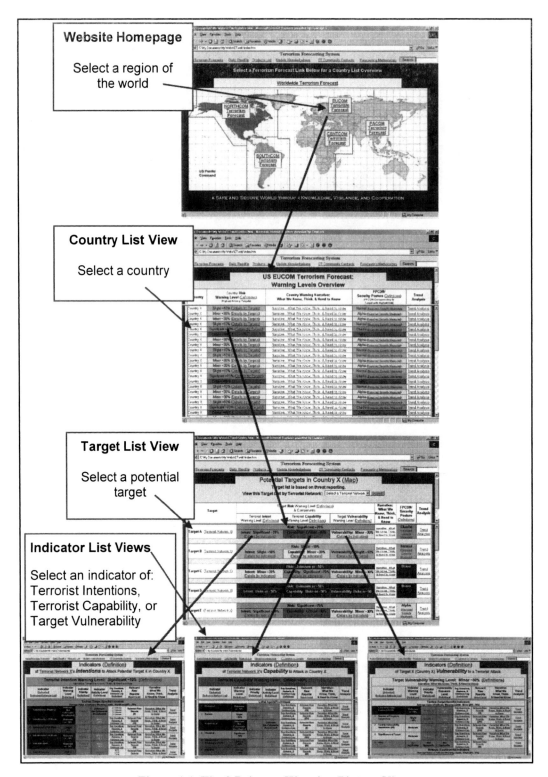

Figure 1.1. The 3 Primary Warning Picture Views

Map from "Unified Command Plan 2002 (UCP 02)," *Proposed EUCOM Area of Responsibility Change (AOR),* 1 October 2002, *United States European Command,* www.eucom.mil/AOR/index.htm (12 June 2002).

This methodology consists of 6 phases of forecasting, which is also called Indications & Warning (I&W) in the Intelligence Community. *Six essential elements* of this methodology facilitate the 6 phases of I&W identified in this research: 1) a list of prioritized terrorism *indicators* help analysts define/validate the key elements of the intelligence problem, 2) an *Intelligence Community Master Database* helps analysts consolidate information, 3) webpage *hypothesis matrices* that are automatically populated by the master database help analysts sort information, 4) a partly automated *systematic process that combines intuitive and structured techniques* (hypothesis testing, matrix logic, chronological sorting, and question set guidance) help analysts draw conclusions, 5) *Collection Requests in warning narratives that describe what we know, think, and need to know* help analysts focus collectors on Intelligence Gaps to refine/update conclusions, and 6) *a website display* helps analysts communicate conclusions/provide warning. The value of the 6 essential elements can be appreciated in the context of an analogy to constructing a building, shown in table 1.1.

Table 1.1. Six Phases of I&W with Corresponding Essential Elements

6 Phases of Indications & Warning (I&W)	6 Essential Elements with Analogy to Constructing a Building
I. Define/Validate Key Elements of the Intelligence Problem	1. Indicators— The Building Blocks of a Warning Assessment
II. Consolidate Information	2. Master Database— The Location to Lay All the Building Blocks
III. Sort Information	3. Hypothesis Matrices— The Blueprint of a Warning Assessment
IV. Draw Conclusions	4. Systematic Process that Combines Intuitive and Structured Techniques— The Tools to Build the Blocks
V. Focus Collectors on Intelligence Gaps to Refine/Update Conclusions	5. Collection Requests in Warning Narratives that Describe What We Know, Think, and Need to Know— Additional Pieces Needed to Fill Gaps In the Building
VI. Communicate Conclusions/Give Warning	6. The Website Display— The Building

Ultimately, just as a building should guard against its common hazards (such as earthquakes), a warning methodology should guard against common warning pitfalls. This methodology guards against 33 of the 42 common warning pitfalls, provides a partial guard against 3 pitfalls, and provides no guard against 6 pitfalls, as shown in table 1.2.

Table 1.2. Six Phases of I&W with Corresponding Essential Elements and Common Warning Pitfalls

6 Phases of Indications & Warning (I&W)	6 Essential Elements with Analogy to Constructing a Building	42 Common Warning Problems/Pitfalls
I. Define/Validate Key Elements of the Intelligence Problem	1. Indicators— The Building Blocks of a Warning Assessment	2 Pitfalls: • Guard against 1 • Partial Guard against 1
II. Consolidate Information	2. Master Database— The Location to Lay All the Building Blocks	2 Pitfalls: • Guard against 1 • No Guard against 1
III. Sort Information	3. Hypothesis Matrices— The Blueprint of a Warning Assessment	9 Pitfalls: • Guard against 9
IV. Draw Conclusions	4. Systematic Process that Combines Intuitive and Structured Techniques— The Tools to Build the Blocks	15 Pitfalls: • Guard against 12 • Partial Guard against 1 • No Guard against 2
V. Focus Collectors on Intelligence Gaps to Refine/Update Conclusions	5. Collection Requests in Warning Narratives that Describe What We Know, Think, and Need to Know— Additional Pieces Needed to Fill Gaps In the Building	2 Pitfalls: • Guard Against 2
VI. Communicate Conclusions/Warning	6. The Website Display— The Building	12 Pitfalls: • Guard against 7 • Partial Guard against 2 • No Guard against 3

This chapter explains the methodology using 23 tasks and the 6 phases of I&W, shown in table 1.3 (Overview of Tasks in Methodology). The 23 tasks include 14 daily tasks, 3 monthly tasks, 4 annual tasks, and 2 as-required tasks. The 14 daily tasks can be completed in 1 day because tasks have been automated wherever possible.[1] Three types of analysts are required to operate this methodology: *Raw Reporting Profilers*, *Indicator Specialists*, and *Senior Warning Officers*. Their responsibilities are described in their corresponding tasks and in the Staffing Plan at the end of this chapter. This methodology could be applied to any intelligence topic (not just terrorism) by simply changing the list of indicators.

Table 1.3. Overview of Tasks in Methodology

Task Set	Phase I: Define/Validate Key Elements of the Intelligence Problem (Using Indicators)
1	Identify/Validate Indicators (Annually)
2	Determine/Validate Priorities of Indicators (Annually)
3	Develop/Validate Key Question Sets on Each Indicator (Annually)
4	Determine/Validate Priorities of Questions in Key Question Sets (Annually)
Task Set	**Phase II: Consolidate Information (Using Master Database)**
5	Intelligence Community Master Database Receives *All* Raw Intelligence Reports from Intelligence Collectors (Daily)
Task Set	**Phase III: Sort Information (Using Hypothesis Matrices)**
6	Enter *All Terrorism Related* Raw Intelligence Reports into Terrorism Forecasting Database Under Appropriate Indicators, Key Questions, Targets, Countries, Terrorist Groups, and Other Data Profile Elements (Daily)
7	Terrorism Forecasting Database Creates *Potential Target Hypothesis Matrices* with Raw Intelligence Reports Filed by Indicators (Daily)
8	Terrorism Forecasting Database Feeds Raw Intelligence Reports into Appropriate *Indicator Key Questions, Answers, & Evidence Logs* within the Hypothesis Matrices (Daily)
9	Assess Raw Intelligence Reports' *Information Validity* (Daily)
Task Set	**Phase IV: Draw Conclusions (Using Intuitive and Structured Techniques)**
10	Assess *Indicator Warning Levels* (Daily)
11	Assess *Terrorist Intention Warning Level* (Daily)
12	Assess *Terrorist Capability Warning Level* (Daily)
13	Assess *Target Vulnerability Warning Level* (Daily)
14	Assess *Target Risk Warning Level* (Daily)
15	Assess *Country Risk Warning Level* (Daily)
16	Update/Study Trend Analysis of Indicator Warning Levels (Monthly)
17	Update/Study Trend Analysis of Target Risk Warning Levels (Monthly)
18	Update/Study Trend Analysis of Country Risk Warning Levels (Monthly)
Task Set	**Phase V: Focus Collectors On Intelligence Gaps to Refine/Update Conclusions (Using Narratives that Describe What We Know, Think, and Need to Know)**
19	Write/Update *Indicator Warning Narrative: What We Know, Think, & Need to Know* (Daily)
20	Write/Update Executive Summary for *Target Warning Narrative: What We Know, Think, & Need to Know* (Daily)
21	Write/Update Executive Summary for *Country Warning Narrative: What We Know, Think, & Need to Know* (Daily)
Task Set	**Phase VI: Communicate Conclusions/Give Warning (Using Templates in Website)**
22	Brief Decision Maker with Website Templates (As Required)
23	Rebrief Decision Maker with New Evidence in Website Templates (As Required)

Phase I: Define/Validate Key Elements of the Intelligence Problem (Using Indicators)

Task 1: Identify/Validate Indicators (Annually)

This forecasting system is based on indicators. Indicators are "those [collectable] things that would have to happen and those that would likely happen as [a] scenario unfolded."[2] For a terrorist attack, those would be things like: terrorist travel, weapons movement, terrorist training, target surveillance, and tests of security. This project research has identified 68 Terrorism Indicators, many of which are listed in table 1.4. For security reasons, some indicators are not shown. Allowing terrorists to become aware of these indicators could make it more difficult for U.S. intelligence to collect on the indicators. Revealing a list of Terrorism Indicators would essentially be revealing an intelligence collection plan against terrorism. The indicators were derived primarily from: case studies of terrorist operations, raw intelligence reporting, the Al Qaeda Manual, and interviews and surveys of terrorism analysts.[3]

In task 1 of this methodology, the leading counterterrorism experts meet on at least an annual basis to determine if indicators should be added to or removed from the list. An indicator must be collectable. If U.S. intelligence does not have the capability to collect on an indicator, then there is no point for analysts to watch for activity on that indicator. Therefore, the experts must ensure the indicators are collectable. Table 1.4 identifies which type of intelligence asset is necessary to collect on each indicator. To cover all the indicators, not only are collection assets necessary from all 4 intelligence disciplines—Human Intelligence (HUMINT), Signals Intelligence (SIGINT), Imagery Intelligence (IMINT), and Measurement and Signatures Intelligence (MASINT); but also from counterintelligence (CI), law enforcement, and open sources (unclassified sources outside the Intelligence Community, such as the Internet). All the types of collection assets can cover some indicators, which are marked as "All Source" in table 1.4.

The indicators are divided into 3 primary groups that reflect the 3 essential factors of *risk*. Risk consists of *adversary capability, adversary intentions*, and *target vulnerability*. All 3 factors must exist in order for risk to exist.[4] The goal of terrorism warning analysis is to identify the risk of a terrorist attack occurring, so analysts must identify indicators for the 3 components of risk.[5] Some people in the Intelligence Community may argue that analysts should only assess *threat* (adversary capability and adversary intentions), not risk, because intelligence is traditionally restricted to assessing only *enemy* force information and risk involves assessing *friendly* force information (target vulnerability). But the reality is decision makers need and want to know if a target is vulnerable to a threat. And intelligence analysts are the best people to synthesize enemy threat information and target vulnerability information into a comprehensive risk assessment.

Within each of the 3 risk component groupings, the indicators are further identified as either *Tactical/Target Specific* or *Strategic/Countrywide*. For instance, among the *Terrorist Intention Indicators*, surveillance reveals terrorists' intentions against a specific target, whereas an indicator such as weapons movement just indicates a terrorist attack is brewing somewhere within a country. All the *Terrorist Capability Indicators* are strategic because terrorists' capabilities tend to be consistent throughout a country. The capability indicators are divided into *lethal agent/technique* and *delivery method*.

Table 1.4. Terrorism Indicators

Terrorism Indicators			
Indicators are "those [collectable] things that would have to happen and . . . would likely happen as [a] scenario unfolded." Indicators must be identified for the 3 factors that comprise risk: Adversary Capability, Adversary Intentions, and Target Vulnerability			
Terrorist Capability Indicators			
Strategic (Countrywide) Indicators	**Priority**	**Data Type**	**Primary Collector**
Lethal Agent/Technique			
1. Biological	1	Qualitative	All Source
2. Nuclear	1	Qualitative	All Source
3. Radiological	2	Qualitative	All Source
4. Chemical	2	Qualitative	All Source
5. Conventional Bombing/Explosion	2	Qualitative	All Source
6. Hijacking	2	Qualitative	All Source
7. Hostage Taking/Kidnapping	2	Qualitative	All Source
8. Assassination	3	Qualitative	All Source
9. Firearms	3	Qualitative	All Source
10. Knives/Blades	3	Qualitative	All Source
11. Computer Network Attack (CNA)	3	Qualitative	All Source
12. Miscellaneous*	NA	Qualitative	All Source
Delivery Method	**Priority**	**Data Type**	**Primary Collector**
13. Ground-Based Vehicle	NA	Qualitative	All Source
14. Water Vessel/Scuba	NA	Qualitative	All Source
15. Aircraft	NA	Qualitative	All Source
16. Missile, Surface-to-Surface	NA	Qualitative	All Source
17. Missile, Surface-to-Air	NA	Qualitative	All Source
18. Missile, Air-to-Surface	NA	Qualitative	All Source
19. Missile, Air-to-Air	NA	Qualitative	All Source
20. Missile, Unknown Type	NA	Qualitative	All Source
21. Suicide Terrorist/Human Host	NA	Qualitative	All Source
22. Mail/Post	NA	Qualitative	All Source
23. Food/Beverages/Water Supply	NA	Qualitative	All Source
24. Gaseous	NA	Qualitative	All Source
25. Miscellaneous*	NA	Qualitative	All Source
Terrorist Intention Indicators			
Strategic (Countrywide) Indicators	**Priority**	**Data Type**	**Primary Collector**
26. Weapons/Material Movement	1	Qualitative	CI, HUMINT
27. Terrorist Travel	1	Qualitative	CI, HUMINT
28. Intentionally Left Blank	1	Qualitative	HUMINT, SIGINT
29. Intentionally Left Blank	1	Qualitative	CI, HUMINT
30. Terrorist Training	1	Qualitative	All Source
31. Anti-Indicators	1 or Trump	Qualitative	All Source
32. Intentionally Left Blank	2	Qualitative	CI
33. Intentionally Left Blank	2	Qualitative	CI, Law Enforcement
34. Intentionally Left Blank	2	Qualitative	CI
35. Intentionally Left Blank	2	Qualitative	HUMINT, SIGINT
36. Intentionally Left Blank	2	Qualitative	SIGINT
37. Intentionally Left Blank	3	Qualitative	Open Source
38. Intentionally Left Blank	3	Qualitative	CI
39. Intentionally Left Blank	3	Qualitative	All Source
40. Significant Events & Dates in Next 30 Days	3	Qualitative	All Source
41. Intentionally Left Blank	3	Qualitative	HUMINT, Open Source
42. Propaganda Levels	3	Qualitative	Open Source
43. Miscellaneous*	NA	Qualitative	All Source

Continued on next page

Table 1.4. Terrorism Indicators Continued

Tactical (Target-Specific) Indicators	Priority	Data Type	Primary Collector
44. Surveillance, Physical	1	Quantitative	CI, Law Enforcement
45. Intentionally Left Blank	1	Qualitative	CI, Law Enforcement
46. Intentionally Left Blank	1	Qualitative	CI, HUMINT, SIGINT
47. Intentionally Left Blank	1	Qualitative	HUMINT, SIGINT
48. Anti-Indicators	1 or Trump	Qualitative	All Source
49. Test of Security	2	Quantitative	CI, Law Enforcement
50. Intentionally Left Blank	2	Quantitative	CI, Law Enforcement
51. Intentionally Left Blank	2	Qualitative	CI, Law Enforcement
52. Intentionally Left Blank	2	Qualitative	CI
53. Intentionally Left Blank	3	Quantitative	CI, Law Enforcement
54. Intentionally Left Blank	3	Qualitative	Open Source
55. Intentionally Left Blank	3	Quantitative	CI, Law Enforcement
56. Intentionally Left Blank	3	Qualitative	CI
57. Intentionally Left Blank	3	Quantitative	CI, Law Enforcement
58. Miscellaneous*	NA	Qualitative	All Source
Target Vulnerability Indicators			
Tactical (Target-Specific) Indicators	Priority	Data Type	Primary Collector
59. Current Security Posture/FPCON	1	Qualitative	CI
60. Number of People in Target Area (Damage Level Capacity)	1	Qualitative	CI
61. Facility Vulnerability Assessment (VA)	2	Qualitative	CI
62. Significance of Target	3	Qualitative	CI
63. Miscellaneous*	NA	Qualitative	All Source
Strategic (Countrywide) Indicators	Priority	Data Type	Primary Collector
64. Country's Ability to Deter and Disrupt Terrorist Activity	1	Qualitative	CI
65. Country's Intent to Deter and Disrupt Terrorist Activity	1	Qualitative	CI
66. Country's Cooperation with the U.S.	2	Qualitative	CI
67. Significant Events & Dates in Next 30 Days	2	Qualitative	CI
68. Miscellaneous*	NA	Qualitative	All Source
*The Miscellaneous Indicators guard against the warning pitfall that indicators cause analysts to discard pertinent kinds of information they did not foresee. Terrorism experts review reports in the miscellaneous categories annually to determine if any new indicators should be established.			

Indicator definition from James J. McDevitt, *Summary of Indicator-Based-Methodology*, unpublished handout, n.p., n.d. provided in January 2002 from the Joint Military Intelligence Training Center.

The indicators are also identified as either quantitative or qualitative for analysis purposes later in the methodology. Quantitative indicators relate to information that can be counted. For example, analysts can count the number of unresolved cases of surveillance at a facility over a given period of time. Qualitative indicators relate to information that cannot be counted, such as terrorist training or propaganda. A great deal of intelligence information is qualitative and must be assessed using intuition since it cannot be counted. However, since intuition is a less accurate method of assessment than numerical calculation, analysts should identify quantitative intelligence information whenever possible, so it can be assessed more accurately via numerical calculations. Seven of the 68 Terrorism Indicators identified in table 1.4 are quantitative.

Notice that there are *Miscellaneous Indicators* within each of the groupings. This is because a list of indicators should never be considered final and comprehensive. Changes in terrorists' modus operandi can lead them to conduct new activities that the U.S. can collect against. Furthermore, changes in U.S. collection capabilities can enable the U.S. to collect on terrorist activities that the U.S. previously could not. Since terrorists will continue to adjust their methods to overcome improvements in security, and since the U.S. will continue to improve (and in some cases lose) collection capabilities with new technology, analysts must periodically review and revise their list of indicators. A method for analysts to keep up with the changes is to use Miscellaneous Indicators to file reports/*indications* that do not fit into any of the existing indicators. (Indications are activities that *have happened* that fall into 1 of the indicator categories.)

Thus, to determine if the list of indicators should be altered, analysts:

1. Review the raw intelligence reports filed under the Miscellaneous Indicators to determine if any kinds of significant terrorist activity have been overlooked.

2. Review U.S. collection capabilities to determine if the U.S. has gained or lost the capability to collect on any terrorist activities.

3. Review case studies of terrorist operations to identify changes in terrorist modus operandi and determine if terrorists are conducting any new activities against which U.S. intelligence can collect.

As analysts create the list of indicators according to that process, they record their rationale and supporting sources for each indicator on the *Indicators-Rationale Log* webpage shown in figure 1.2.

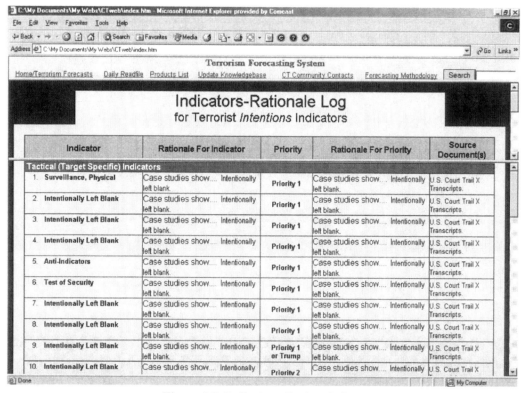

Figure 1.2. Indicators-Rationale Log

Task 2: Determine/Validate Priorities of Indicators (Annually)

Some indicators are more significant than others. For instance, among the indicators of terrorist intentions, *weapons movement* to the target area must take place before an attack; whereas an increase in terrorist *propaganda* is not a prerequisite. Therefore, weapons movement would carry a higher significance/priority than increased propaganda. Likewise, some capability indicators reflect a greater damage potential than others. For instance, a nuclear attack will kill more people than a conventional bombing. Therefore, nuclear attack would carry a higher priority. Similarly, some vulnerability indicators can have a greater effect on a target's vulnerability than others. For instance, a location's Force Protection Condition (FPCON/security posture) has a higher effect on a facility's vulnerability than the level of the country's cooperation with the U.S. *Indicator Priority* is an intuitive rating on the significance of an indicator.

On at least an annual basis, the leading counterterrorism experts determine if the priority of any of the indicators needs to be adjusted. The indicators are prioritized in this methodology on a scale of 1 through 3 according to the following definitions.

Terrorist Intention Indicators

Priority 1: Those things that *must* occur (about 99 percent) before an attack.
Priority 2: Those things that are *highly likely* (about 80 percent) to occur before an attack.
Priority 3: Those things that are *likely* (about 60 percent) to occur before an attack.

Keep in mind that priority is based on the analyst's assessment that the activity is likely or must *occur* before an attack. Priority does *not* reflect the likelihood that intelligence will *detect and collect* on the activity. Task 10 describes how the methodology accounts for the fact that the U.S. cannot collect on certain indicators at certain locations.

Terrorist Capability Indicators

Priority 1: Capabilities that are *most likely* to have *high* damage on a population (more than 10,000 people).
Priority 2: Capabilities that are *most likely* to have *moderate* damage on a population (more than 100 and less than 10,000 people).
Priority 3: Capabilities that are *most likely* to have *low* damage on a population (less than 100 people).

The "most likely" is a key point. Notice that *Computer Network Attack* is rated as a *Priority 3 Indicator*. Of course it is foreseeable that a computer network attack could have a devastating effect on a population, but the reality is that computer network attacks occur daily and are currently most likely to have low damage on a population. The priority of an indicator can be changed at any time.

Target Vulnerability Indicators

Priority 1: Those things that have a *high* effect (about 90 percent) on the vulnerability of a target.
Priority 2: Those things that have a *moderate* effect (about 50 percent) on the vulnerability of a target.
Priority 3: Those things that have a *low* effect (about 10 percent) on the vulnerability of a target.

As analysts determine the priorities of the indicators according to these guidelines, they also record their rationale and supporting sources for each indicator priority on the Indicators-Rationale Log (already shown in figure 1.2).

Task 3: Develop/Validate Key Question Sets on Each Indicator (Annually)

Since indicators are the foundation and building blocks of this methodology, the type of information required to assess the status of an indicator should be clearly defined and recorded. Thus, on at least an annual basis, the leading counterterrorism experts validate a list of key questions for each indicator. The question sets identify the key factors that experts have determined are necessary to assess the status of a given indicator.

For instance, U.S. court case records show that Muslim extremist terrorist operatives who conduct the long-term planning of a terrorist attack tend to travel into the target country with valid passports and detailed cover stories; whereas the terrorist operatives who actually carry out the attack tend to travel into the country just several days before the attack without valid passports or detailed cover stories.[6] Therefore, a Priority 1 question for the *Terrorist Travel Indicator* might be, "Have any terrorist operatives attempted to travel into the country without valid passports or detailed cover stories?"

Not only do these question sets serve to assist an analyst in assessing the status of an indicator, but they also serve as the prioritized Collection Requirements for intelligence collectors. The entire list of indicators and corresponding key question sets form an intelligence collection plan against terrorism. These questions define what the Counterterrorism Community needs to know in order to recognize when a terrorist attack operation is unfolding and how to stop it. As collectors provide analysts the answers to these questions, analysts will be able to assess the indicators of a terrorist attack.

The questions must be stated in a particular format so they meet the needs of both intelligence collectors and analysts, and so that they are compatible with automated functions later in the methodology, which will save analysts time. A question on a key factor must first be stated in a yes/no question format, such as "Have any terrorist operatives attempted to travel into the country without valid passports or detailed cover stories?" Then the question should be broken into subquestions that require collectors to provide details, such as "Who were the suspected terrorists? When did they arrive? What was their cover story? How did they obtain the false passports? Who were they supposed to meet? Do they know of any other terrorists who will also try to enter the country?" Table 1.5 shows this format for a given indicator.

Table 1.5. Indicator Key Question-Set Format

#	Priority	Question
		**Key Questions for Indicator X**

#	Priority	Question
1	1	What is the first key factor to consider in assessing this indicator? How do you state a question on this key factor in a yes/no question format?
1a		▪ What details do you need on this key factor?
1b		▪ What other details do you need on this key factor?
1c		▪ What other details do you need on this key factor?
2	1	What is the second key factor to consider in assessing this indicator? How do you state a question on this key factor in a yes/no question format?
2a		▪ What details do you need on this key factor?
2b		▪ What other details do you need on this key factor?
2c		▪ What other details do you need on this key factor?
3	2	What is the third key factor to consider in assessing this indicator? How do you state a question on this key factor in a yes/no question format?
3a		▪ What details do you need on this key factor?
3b		▪ What other details do you need on this key factor?
3c		▪ What other details do you need on this key factor?
4	3	What is the fourth key factor to consider in assessing this indicator? How do you state a question on this key factor in a yes/no question format?
4a		▪ What details do you need on this key factor?
4b		▪ What other details do you need on this key factor?
4c		▪ What other details do you need on this key factor?

As analysts create the list of questions according to those guidelines, they record their rationale and supporting sources for each question on the *Indicator Key Questions-Rationale Log* webpage shown in figure 1.3.

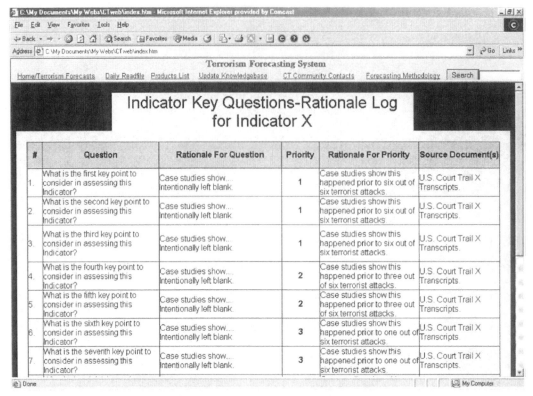

Figure 1.3. Indicator Key Questions-Rationale Log

Task 4: Determine/Validate Priorities of Questions in Key Question Sets (Annually)

The leading counterterrorism experts also prioritize the key questions on a scale of 1 through 3 with 1 being the most significant. Only the yes/no format questions need to be prioritized, as already shown in table 1.5 (Indicator Key Question Set Format). These priorities affect both intelligence collection priorities and analysts' assessments. As analysts determine the priorities of the questions, they also record their rationale and supporting sources for each question priority on the Indicator Key Questions-Rationale Log (already shown in figure 1.3).

Phase II: Consolidate Information (Using Master Database)

Task 5: Intelligence Community Master Database Receives *All* Raw Intelligence Reports from Intelligence Collectors (Daily)

The daily process begins with the requirement that all fifteen Member Organizations of the Intelligence Community [Air Force Intelligence, Army Intelligence, Central Intelligence Agency

(CIA), Coast Guard Intelligence, Defense Intelligence Agency (DIA), Department of Energy, Department of Homeland Security (DHS), Department of State, Department of Treasury, Federal Bureau of Investigation (FBI), Marine Corps Intelligence, National Geospatial-Intelligence Agency (NGA), National Reconnaissance Office (NRO), National Security Agency (NSA), and Navy Intelligence][7] and other U.S. federal organizations that may have terrorism-related information [such as the National Infrastructure Protection Center (NIPC), the Center For Disease Control (CDC), and the Drug Enforcement Administration (DEA)] forward *all* their raw intelligence reports (on all intelligence topics, not just terrorism) to an *Intelligence Community Master Database.* Based on the field headings that intelligence collectors put on the reports, the reports are automatically filed in the database according to identification number, classification, and broad intelligence topics such as terrorism or economics. (A report can relate to more than 1 topic.) Additionally, the FBI would consolidate suspicious incident reports from local law enforcement agencies, private security companies, commercial firms, and private citizens to forward to the database. Each agency can sanitize their reports (remove information that may compromise sensitive sources and methods or reveal the identity of U.S. citizens) before sending them to the database. If sanitizing a report will remove the threat information, then the report is classified at a level that causes the database to restrict access to only a limited number of analysts and system administrators. Thus the database restricts a user's access to individual reports based on both the user's identification and the report's classification.

Consolidating all raw intelligence reporting is a critical task because fractionalized distribution of information was cited as a key cause of warning failure in 2 of the United State's most devastating homeland surprise attacks—Pearl Harbor and the September 11 terrorist attacks. No less than 6 Pearl Harbor inquiries cited the problem over fifty years ago. Yet the problem still persists today. There is no single database that consolidates all the Intelligence Community's raw reporting. The Director of Central Intelligence (DCI) should mandate that all Member Organizations of the Intelligence Community send copies of all their raw reporting to a single Intelligence Community Master Database. That would enable any organization monitoring a given topic, such as terrorism, to draw all the necessary reporting from 1 database. Today, terrorism analysts would have to gain access to at least 6 different databases to get all terrorism-related raw intelligence reporting. Understandably there is a need to compartmentalize some information in order to protect sensitive sources and methods. Today's Information Technology is capable of restricting access within a database based on both a report's classification and a user's identification. The major benefit of hindsight after intelligence warning failures is that it is the first time all the information has been consolidated. Of course analysts need all available pieces of a puzzle to make the best possible assessment.

Phase III: Sort Information (Using Hypothesis Matrices)

Task 6: Enter *All Terrorism Related* Raw Intelligence Reports into Terrorism Forecasting Database Under Appropriate Indicators, Key Questions, Targets, Countries, Terrorist Groups, and Other Data Profile Elements (Daily)

Now that analysts have: 1) received all the raw intelligence reporting (in 1 database), and 2) defined the kind of information that is important for terrorism warning/forecasting (the indicators and key questions), the analysts can begin their first daily task, which is simply to profile/enter incoming reports into a terrorism forecasting-specific database according to the indicators, key questions, targets, countries, terrorist groups, and other terrorism forecasting-specific data profile elements identified in figure 1.4. (That procedure could be done for any intelligence-forecasting topic, not just terrorism.) This secondary level database is necessary because the Intelligence Community Master Database would become too complex if it contained all the forecasting-specific data profile elements for terrorism and every other intelligence topic. Every forecasting topic has a different set of forecasting-specific data profile elements. Furthermore, if the Intelligence Community Master Database were also used to file reports according to forecasting-specific data profile elements, then the database could not have *functional integrity* for those terrorism forecasting-specific data profile elements. For a database to have functional integrity, it must, for example, be able to make certain data profile elements mandatory entries when new information is entered into the database. However, the Intelligence Community Master Database could make no such requirement for terrorism-specific data profile elements because the database automatically accepts new raw intelligence reports from intelligence collectors according to only the more broad intelligence topics they are required to identify. Analysts require time, critical thinking, and the leeway to change the profile of a raw intelligence report at any time according to forecasting-specific data profile elements. Functional integrity is a key reason for creating databases, and it also drives automatic processes later in this forecasting methodology. Therefore, a secondary database is necessary to establish functional integrity for the forecasting-specific data. Thus, the Intelligence Community Master Database functions like a queue to consolidate and hold the raw intelligence reports according to nonspecific data profile elements until analysts have a chance to profile the reports according to specific data profile elements.

In this task of the methodology, a large group of junior analysts, called *Raw Reporting Profilers*, reads through the Intelligence Community Master Database's incoming terrorism-related raw intelligence reports (an estimated 2500 per day,[8] which are already marked as terrorism related) and enters *all* of them into a *Terrorism Forecasting Database* under the data profile elements shown in figure 1.4, which shows the input form for the database. (A partial list of the data profile elements, which includes the corresponding drop down menus, is available on the CD under the hyperlink "Update Knowledgebase." The list excludes some data profile elements for security reasons.)

Profiling a typical report according to these factors is as simple as checking a list of boxes in the database drop down menus, and it takes about 10 minutes to profile a report. (A report's classification profile from the Intelligence Community Master Database automatically carries over to the Terrorism Forecasting Database, so access to the report within the forecasting database is again restricted based on both the report's classification and a user's identification.) When entering a report into the master database, the Raw Reporting Profilers check the lists of boxes to indicate all the terrorist groups, countries, specific targets, indicators, and key questions that apply to the report. A single raw report may relate to multiple terrorist groups, countries, specific targets, indicators, and key questions. If a report does not fit into any of the existing indicators, the analyst files the report in the appropriate *Other/Miscellaneous* terrorist intention, terrorist capability, or target vulnerability indicator. If a report pertains to a target or terrorist group that is not listed, the analyst can add the target or terrorist group to the list.

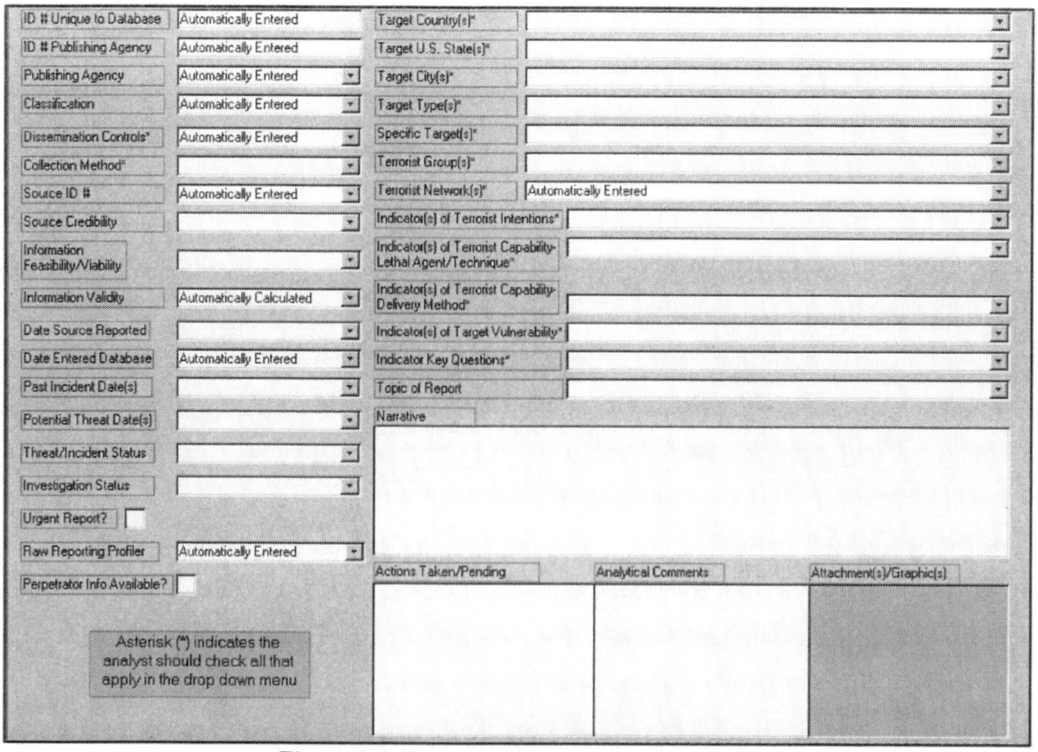

ID # Unique to Database	Automatically Entered		Target Country(s)*		▼
ID # Publishing Agency	Automatically Entered		Target U.S. State(s)*		▼
Publishing Agency	Automatically Entered	▼	Target City(s)*		▼
Classification	Automatically Entered	▼	Target Type(s)*		▼
Dissemination Controls*	Automatically Entered	▼	Specific Target(s)*		▼
Collection Method*		▼	Terrorist Group(s)*		▼
Source ID #	Automatically Entered	▼	Terrorist Network(s)*	Automatically Entered	▼
Source Credibility		▼	Indicator(s) of Terrorist Intentions*		▼
Information Feasibility/Viability		▼	Indicator(s) of Terrorist Capability-Lethal Agent/Technique*		▼
Information Validity	Automatically Calculated	▼	Indicator(s) of Terrorist Capability-Delivery Method*		▼
Date Source Reported		▼	Indicator(s) of Target Vulnerability*		▼
Date Entered Database	Automatically Entered	▼	Indicator Key Questions*		▼
Past Incident Date(s)		▼	Topic of Report		▼
Potential Threat Date(s)		▼	Narrative		
Threat/Incident Status		▼			
Investigation Status		▼			
Urgent Report? □					
Raw Reporting Profiler	Automatically Entered	▼			
Perpetrator Info Available? □			Actions Taken/Pending	Analytical Comments	Attachment(s)/Graphic(s)

Asterisk (*) indicates the analyst should check all that apply in the drop down menu

Figure 1.4. Terrorism Forecasting Database
Raw Intelligence Report Input Form
Source: created by author with assistance from Tandra Turner, Erin Whitworth, and Gurumeet Kaur Khalsa.[9]

Using an artificial intelligence computer program to presort the 2500 reports based on key words could reduce the number of analysts required to do this task. These programs are about 80 percent accurate according to research. Humans are also about 80 percent accurate according to research.[10] By combining both, analysts can increase accuracy and save time and manpower.

Task 7: Terrorism Forecasting Database Creates *Potential Target Hypothesis Matrices* with Raw Intelligence Reports Filed by Indicators (Daily)

After analysts enter raw intelligence reports into the master database, the computer program automatically creates *Potential Target Hypothesis Matrix* webpages (as shown in figure 1.5, Hypothesis Matrix: Indicator List View) and displays hyperlinks to the reports under the appropriate indicator(s) within the hypothesis matrices. The hypothesis matrix in figure 1.5 shows the indicators and indications of a terrorist network's intentions to attack a target in a given country. This hypothesis matrix lists just the Terrorist *Intention* Indicators from top to bottom, with those that are of a tactical (or target-specific) nature grouped on the top and those of a strategic (or country-wide) nature grouped off the screen on the bottom. Notably, a terrorist network includes multiple groups that cooperate or use each other's resources. Thus a hypothesis matrix can include reporting on multiple terrorist groups within the same terrorist network. (By clicking on the "Terrorist Network" hyperlink, users can see which terrorist groups are included in this terrorist network and hypothesis matrix.)

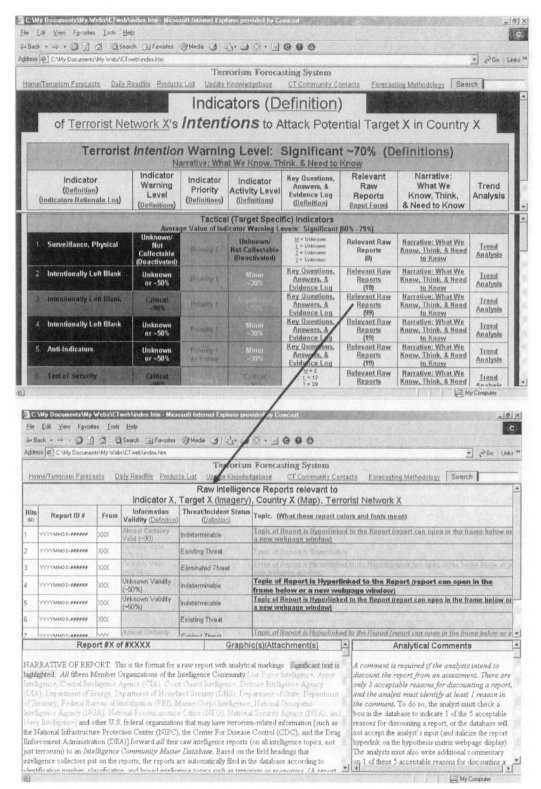

Figure 1.5. Hypothesis Matrix: Indicator List View (with Link to Raw Reports Display)

"Analysis of competing hypotheses" (which compares evidence of what must happen and is likely to happen for potential scenarios) has been identified as "one of the most valuable techniques for determining the scale of a threat."[11] Each matrix lays out hyperlinks to all the evidence or *raw intelligence reports* relating to that hypothesis. The reports/evidence are grouped by their level of *Information Validity* (discussed further in task 9) and then the reports are listed in chronological order with the most current on top within each of those validity groupings. The levels of Information Validity are: 1) *Almost Certainly Valid (~90%)*, about 90 percent probability, 2) *Probably Valid (~70%)*, 3) *Unknown Validity (or ~50%)*, 4) *Probably Not Valid (~30%)*, and 5) *Almost Certainly Not Valid (~10%)*. Analysts can change the list to simply most current on top if they want. Some report hyperlinks do not lead to the text of the report in order protect especially sensitive intelligence sources and methods; instead, the hyperlink leads to the contact information of the database security manager, who can provide the report to people with a need to know.

It is 2 times more effective to disprove a hypothesis than to prove one.[12] For that reason, *Anti-Indicators* are also maintained in each hypothesis matrix to file reports that are inconsistent with the hypothesis. To identify Anti-Indicators analysts should ask themselves questions like: What would make me change my mind? What is missing that is essential?[13] What would prevent this scenario from unfolding? What has happened that would not happen before a terrorist attack? Unlike typical hypothesis testing that discards a hypothesis with 1 piece of refuting evidence,[14] this methodology does not because intelligence information is not necessarily credible and that understanding must be factored into assessments accordingly. The refuting information is either weighed as a *Priority 1* indicator, or the analyst can negate the hypothesis if the information is deemed highly credible. The analyst decides on a case-by-case basis and the indicator is marked on the webpage as either *Priority 1* or *Trump*. Weighing the value of evidence, whether it is consistent or inconsistent with a hypothesis, is acceptable with intelligence information because intelligence information is not as reliable as scientific information obtained in controlled experiments. Thus, with intelligence information, "the analyst selects the hypothesis that seems best supported by the evidence."[15]

If a report of about 50 percent validity or greater arrives that pertains to a target, country, or terrorist network that has not been previously reported, then the computer program automatically creates a new hypothesis matrix to represent that target, country, or terrorist network when the analyst enters the report into the database. Thus, the reporting drives development of new threat scenarios/hypotheses. This guards against the indicator-based warning pitfall that "scenarios create mindsets," which can cause analysts to discard reporting that points to an unimagined threat scenario/hypothesis.

Task 8: Terrorism Forecasting Database Feeds Raw Intelligence Reports into Appropriate *Indicator Key Questions, Answers, & Evidence Logs* within the Hypothesis Matrices (Daily)

The master database also feeds the raw reports into the appropriate *Indicator Key Questions, Answers, & Evidence Logs* within the Hypothesis Matrices, as shown in figure 1.6. Thus a hyperlink to a given raw report exists in both a hypothesis matrix and an *Indicator Key Questions, Answers, & Evidence Log*, which contains the key question sets identified in task 3.

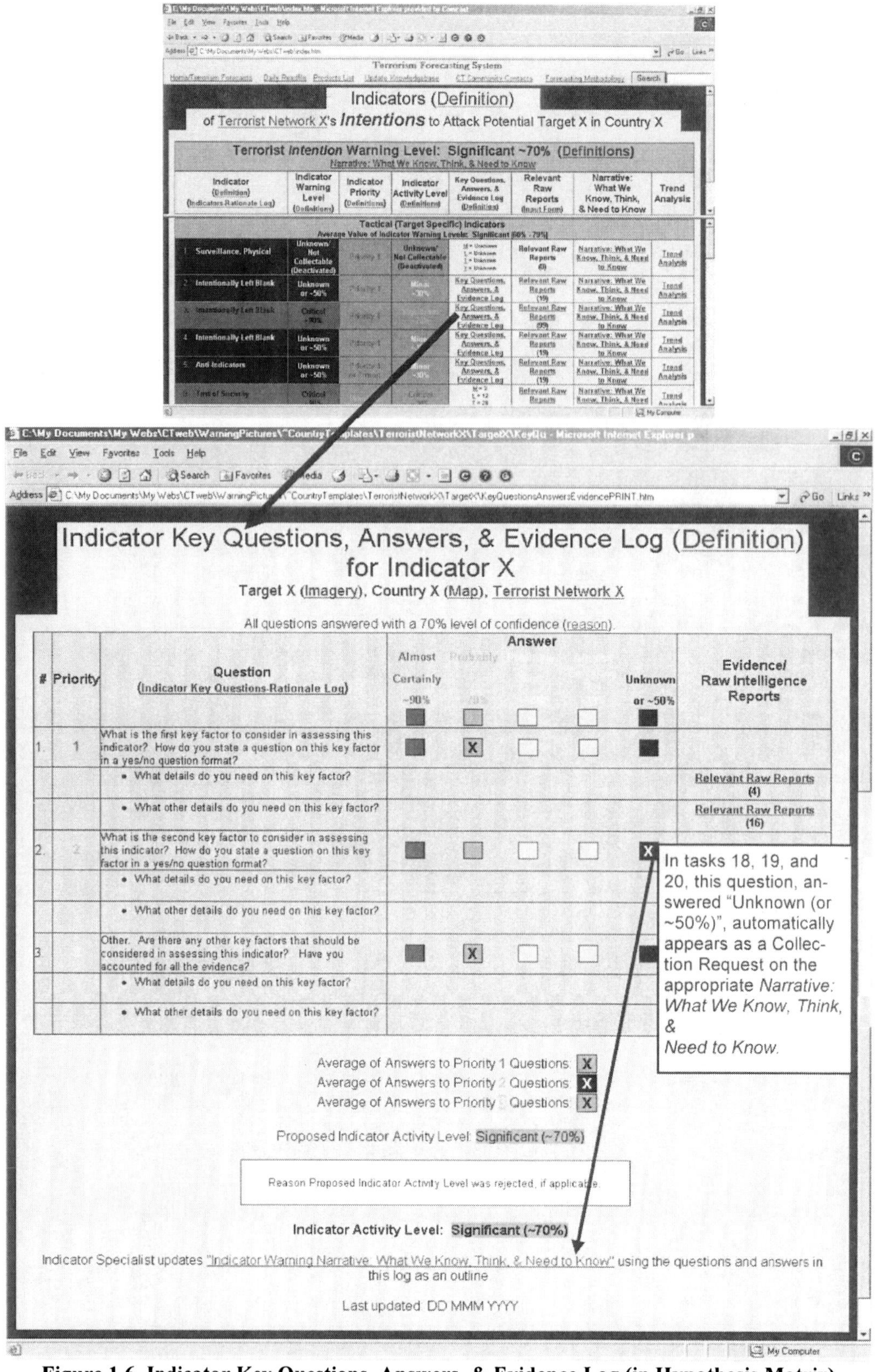

Figure 1.6. Indicator Key Questions, Answers, & Evidence Log (in Hypothesis Matrix)

Task 9: Assess Raw Intelligence Reports' *Information Validity* (Daily)

Notice that the report hyperlinks are color coded in figure 1.5 [Hypothesis Matrix: Indicator List View (with Link to Raw Reports Display)].[16] As analysts profile a report in the database, they check a list of boxes to rate *Source Credibility* [on a 5-level scale of 1) "Almost Certainly Credible (~90%)," about 90 percent probability, 2) "Probably Credible (~70%)," 3) "Probably Not Credible (~30%)," 4) "Almost Certainly Not Credible (~10%)," and 5) "Unknown Credibility (or ~50%)"] and *Information Feasibility/Viability* [on a 5-level scale of 1) "Almost Certainly Feasible/Viable (~90%)," about 90 percent probability, 2) "Probably Feasible/Viable (~70%)," 3) "Probably Not Feasible/Viable (~30%)," 4) "Almost Certainly Not Feasible/Viable (~10%)," and 5) "Unknown Feasibility/Viability (or ~50%)"]. Then the computer program uses those values to calculate the report's *Information Validity* via *Utility Matrix 1*, shown in figure 1.7.

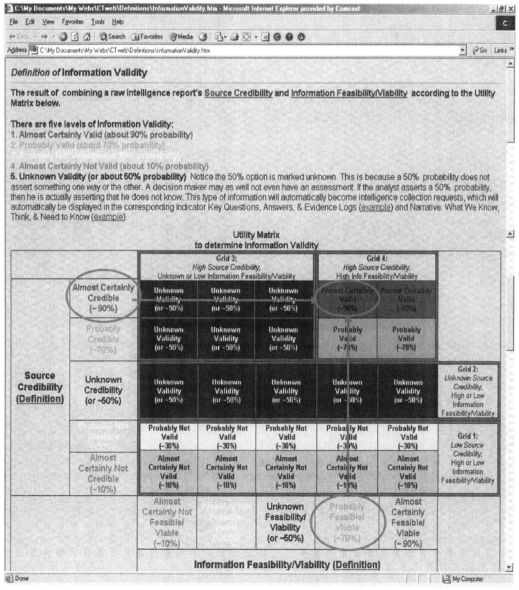

Figure 1.7. Utility Matrix 1

This is how Utility Matrix 1 works. The computer application combines the Source Credibility (shown on the y-axis of Figure 1.7. Utility Matrix 1) and the Information Viability (shown on the x-axis of Figure 1.7. Utility Matrix 1) according to Utility Matrix 1 to determine the Information Validity on a 5-level scale of 1) "Almost Certainly Valid (~90%)," about 90 percent probability, 2) "Probably Valid (~70%)," 3) "Probably Not Valid (~30%)," 4) "Almost Certainly Not Valid (~10%)," and 5) "Unknown Validity (or ~50%)." For instance, if the intelligence collector had judged the source as "Almost Certainly Credible (~90%)," and the analyst had judged the information as "Probably Feasible/Viable (~70%)," then the Information Validity would be "Almost Certainly Valid (~90%)." The resulting value is indicated by a red hyperlink on the website display, as already shown in figure 1.5 [Hypothesis Matrix: Indicator List View (with Link to Raw Reports Display)].

Rationale and Actions to Take

The rationales to determine Information Validity from Source Credibility and Information Feasibility/Viability fall into four primary categories, which are identified by four grids marked on the utility matrix: Grid 1, Grid 2, Grid 3, and Grid 4. Each grid also corresponds to the action an analyst should take on the information. The calculations to determine Information Validity from Source Credibility and Information Feasibility/Viability are automated, but the actions the analyst should take are not. The actions are geared toward determining whether the information should be briefed to a decision maker.

1. Grid 1: If Source Credibility is low (about 30 percent or lower) and Information Feasibility/Viability is high (about 70 percent or greater) or low (about 30 percent or lower), then Information Validity is low (about 30 percent or lower).

    Rationale: There are infinite threat possibilities/feasibilities, so an analyst must narrow them down by using Source Credibility. When a threat report originates from a source that is only about 30 percent credible or less, the threat should not stand out from among the infinite threat possibilities. Ultimately, Information Validity should not be higher than Source Credibility, regardless of how feasible the information is.

    Action: The information in this grid is not of briefing quality. Neither is the information of the quality to take time to question and apply valuable intelligence resources to search for answers. The analyst should discount the information that falls into this grid/category. The reader may be surprised to learn that analysts receive many reports in this category. These reports are known as "chaff," irrelevant information that can cause an analyst to become overwhelmed if he does not discount it. However, some of the reports of about 30 percent validity should be given consideration if they relate to a significant threat, such as nuclear. Task 10 of the methodology "bumps up" these threats to Intelligence Gaps, which are turned into Collection Requests.

2. Grid 2: If Source Credibility is unknown (about 50 percent) and Information Feasibility/Viability is high (about 70 percent or greater) or low (about 30 percent or lower), then Information Validity is unknown (about 50 percent).

    Rationale: In matters of security, it is best to err on the side of caution, so a threat report that originate from a source of about 50 percent (unknown) credibility should not be discounted since there is a reasonable chance the threat is valid. Sources of unknown (and high) credibility deserve consideration, but sources of low credibility do not because researching them would drain the limited intelligence resources available. In this methodology, a 50 percent probability is the threshold that makes a threat worth intelligence resources.

Action: The analyst is not ready to brief the threat if the source credibility is in question, regardless of how feasible the information is. The analyst needs to request more information on the topic to find out if there are corroborating sources. Additionally, if the information is not feasible, the analyst needs to brainstorm and research the Information Feasibility/Viability; even if the analyst discovers that there are corroborating sources, he still will not be ready to brief if he cannot assert whether the threat is possible.

3. Grid 3: If Source Credibility is high (about 70 percent or greater) and Information Feasibility/Viability is unknown (about 50 percent) or low (about 30 percent or lower), then Information Validity is unknown (about 50 percent).

    Rationale: A highly (about 70 percent or greater) credible source is worth giving consideration regardless of how unfeasible the information seems. An attacker's goal is to surprise its victim because that significantly increases the chance of success. Therefore, an analyst must open his mind to unexpected possibilities that highly credible sources report.

    Action: The analyst is not ready to brief the threat if he cannot even assert whether the threat is possible. The analyst needs to get answers on Information Feasibility/Viability by brainstorming (to opening his mind) and researching to determine if the threat is of briefing quality.

4. Grid 4: If Source Credibility is high (about 70 percent or greater) and Information Feasibility/Viability is high (about 70 percent or greater), then Information Validity is high (about 70 percent or greater).

    Rationale: Obviously information of both high (about 70 percent or greater) Source Credibility and high feasibility/viability has a high probability of being valid.

    Action: This information is of briefing quality and evidence quality (about 70 percent or higher). The analyst should apply the information as supporting evidence in a hypothesis matrix to determine if the combination of multiple pieces of information amount to at least 70 percent of those things that must happen and are likely to happen for a scenario to unfold (indicators). If the the pieces of information (raw intelligence reports) amount to 70 percent of the indicators, then the analyst is ready to brief the decision maker on the threat. Seventy percent was chosen based on Secretary of State Colin Powell's remarks on warning, "what I need to do is operate when the probability of something happening is about, not .2, but about .7. I can't wait until it's .99 because by then it's too late."[17]

Based on those rationales, the computer application determines a report's Information Validity, and groups the lists of reports on the webpages according to the following prioritized order and color-coding system [as already shown in figure 1.5, Hypothesis Matrix: Indicator List View (with Link to Raw Reports Display)]:

1. Red hyperlinks indicate reports that are judged "Almost Certainly Valid (~90%)," about 90 percent probability.
2. Orange hyperlinks indicate reports that are judged "Probably Valid (~70%)."
3. Black hyperlinks indicate reports that are judged "Unknown Validity (or ~50%)." Notice that the 50 percent option is marked unknown. This is because a 50 percent probability does not assert something one way or the other. A decision maker may as well not even have an assessment. If the analyst asserts a 50 percent probability, then he is actually asserting that he does not know.
4. Yellow hyperlinks indicate reports that are judged "Probably Not Valid (~30%)."
5. Gray hyperlinks indicate reports that are judged "Almost Certainly Not Valid (~10%)."

Notice that all gray hyperlinks will also be italicized because they all meet at least one of the criteria for discounting a report (either noncredible source or nonfeasible information).

6. Bold hyperlinks indicate reports that pertain to threats within the next 30 days.
7. Italicized hyperlinks indicate reports that analysts intend to discount from assessments. There are only 5 acceptable reasons to discount a raw intelligence report, and an analyst must identify at least 1 reason in the Terrorism Forecasting Database by checking the appropriate box, or the database will not accept the analyst's input (and italicize the report hyperlink on the website display). The analysts must also write additional commentary in the analytical comment section for the raw intelligence report in the Terrorism Forecasting Database. The five acceptable reasons to discount a raw intelligence report are:

Reason 1: The threat expires. For instance, if a report states that terrorists intend to attack before the end of the New Year, and then the date passes for several months without incident. Choosing to expire a threat can be a difficult decision because terrorists may back off an operation if the conditions become unfavorable, and then to return to the operation once conditions become favorable. In this forecasting system, the computer application automatically expires threats after 90 days and automatically checks the box "Expired Threat" under the data field *Threat/Incident Status* in the Terrorism Forecasting Database.

Reason 2: Officials eliminate the threat. For instance, if FBI officials apprehend a suspected terrorist who had reportedly traveled into the country, then the threat from that terrorist is eliminated. In this forecasting system, an analyst can indicate that a threat has been eliminated by checking the box "Eliminated Threat" under the data field Threat/Incident Status in the Terrorism Forecasting Database.

Reason 3: Officials determine through investigation that the threat/incident was benign. The threat never existed. For instance, if while investigating a reported surveillance of nuclear facility, officials discover that person who took the photograph was part of a government chartered risk assessment team, then the threat is benign. In this forecasting system, an analyst can indicate that a threat is benign by checking the box "Confirmed Benign Threat/Incident" under the data field Threat/Incident Status in the Terrorism Forecasting Database.

Reason 4: The intelligence collector determines that the source is not credible. In some cases, analysts can make a judgment on source credibility, but analysts must remember that in most (not all) cases, the collector knows the source (and his reporting history) better than the analyst. In this forecasting system, an analyst must indicate a source's credibility by checking a box for one of the following options in the Forecasting Database under Source Credibility: 1) Almost Certainly Credible (~90%), about 90 percent probability, 2) Probably Credible (~70%), 3) Probably Not Credible (~30%), 4) Almost Certainly Not Credible (~10%), and 5) Unknown Credibility (or ~50%). If the collector did not describe the source according to those words, then the analyst judges which option best fits the collector's description of the source. The analyst must be 70 percent confident of his answer.

Reason 5: Analysts judged that the information is not feasible/viable; the information does not make logical sense. Analysts must understand that a judgment that an indication does not make sense is different from an opinion that the indication is unlikely, which is not an appropriate reason to dismiss an indication. For instance, on a report of a possible case of photographic surveillance, if the analyst thinks it is unlikely the incident was actually a surveillance incident because the suspect had his family posing on the picturesque hilltop over Camp Doha, Kuwait, then that opinion is not an appropriate reason to dismiss that indication of surveillance. However, if an investigation determines that the camera used did not have a strong enough lens to take a clear picture of Camp Doha from the distance it was taken, then that logic *is* an appropriate reason to dismiss the indication. This is the principle that Department of Defense (DoD) warning analysts apply to selecting potential threat scenarios.[18] Since an indication is like a mini threat scenario, the same principle should apply. In this forecasting system, an analyst must indicate the information's feasibility/viability by checking a box for one of the following options in the Forecasting Database under Information Feasibility/Viability: 1) Almost Certainly Feasible/Viable (~90%), about 90 percent probability, 2) Probably Feasible/Viable (~70%), 3) Probably Not Feasible/Viable (~30%), 4) Almost Certainly Not Feasible/Viable (~10%), and 5) Unknown Feasibility/Viability (or ~50%). The analyst must be 70 percent confident of his answer. An analyst can always discount a report for this reason when the Source Credibility is lower than 50 percent. However, when the Source Credibility is 50 percent or higher, the analyst should put out Collection Requests on the threat topic to confirm that the threat can really be discounted.

Some analysts may fear that the strict guidelines for discounting a report will cause many false alarms (because many reports will not meet the criteria to be discounted). However, as will become apparent in task 11, a warning level does not increase unless multiple indications tied to multiple indicators for a hypothesis amount to enough significance to drive up a warning level. This single task (determining whether to discount a raw report) is subject to 9 common warning pitfalls, 8 of which involve analysts neglecting pertinent information for reasons they believe are justified, but actually are not justified. Thus, analysts must strictly adhere to the 5 guidelines for dismissing indications, and should be trained in their application so they do not mistakenly force the threat picture to meet their prejudice. The threat picture must represent the ground truth of all the legitimate indications that have been reported. The analyst will have a chance to apply his intuition to the information later, but in this step of building the threat picture, the analyst must simply lay out the facts. Indications are the fundamental building blocks of a warning picture, so this step must be done right.

The requirement for an analyst to write out the justification for dismissing an indication according to 1 of the 5 prescribed reasons helps the analyst ensure his reasoning is based on logic rather than bias. Furthermore, the fact that the justification is available on the report for all other analysts to review provides for a system of checks and balances which helps guard against the "serious random [intuitive] inconsistencies" that a person experiences due to personal bias, "fatigue, boredom, and all the factors that make us human."[19]

Notice that no report is ever removed from the list in a hypothesis matrix; rather, it is italicized. Common adversary modus operandi is to back off an operation if conditions become unfavorable and return to the operation once conditions become favorable again.[20] As a result, an analyst may need previous indications to decipher details of a potential operation that has shown renewed activity. Furthermore, maintaining *all* reports (including noncredible, nonfeasible, expired, eliminated, and benign threat reports) on the website display enables everyone within the Counterterrorism Community to be aware of the reports and helps alleviate misunderstandings as to the reports' existence and/or status.

Some reports' hyperlinks do not lead to the text of the report in order protect especially sensitive intelligence sources and methods. Instead, the hyperlink leads to the contact information of the database security manager, who can provide the report to people with a need to know.

Phase IV: Draw Conclusions
(Using Intuitive and Structured Techniques))

Task 10: Assess *Indicator Warning Levels* (Daily)

Now that all the incoming information has been sorted and filed within the hypothesis matrices according to the significant criteria (indicators, targets, countries, and other data profile elements identified in task 6), this next step is done by a second group of analysts who are *Indicator Specialists*. Indicator Specialists are the Counterterrorism Community's designated experts in determining the *Indicator Activity Level* of a given indicator or set of indicators on a 5-level scale of 1) *Critical (~90%)*, about 90 percent probability, color coded red on the website, 2) *Significant (~70%)*, color coded orange, 3) *Minor (~30%)*, color coded yellow, 4) *Slight (~10%)*, color coded gray, and 5) *Unknown (or ~50%)*, color coded black. The analysts do this in 1 of 2 ways.

1) *Determine Indicator Activity Level for Qualitative Indicators Via Indicator Key Questions, Answers, & Evidence Logs*

To determine the *Indicator Activity Level* for the *qualitative* indicators (which relate to information that cannot be counted) an analyst uses the *Indicator Key Questions, Answers, & Evidence Log* (already shown in figure 1.6) to assist him with that intuitive judgment. For each question, the analyst must select 1 of the following 5 answers: 1) "Almost Certainly True (~90%)," about 90 percent probability, color coded red on the website, 2) "Probably True (~70%)," color coded orange, 3) "Probably Not True (~30%)," color coded yellow, 4) "Almost Certainly Not True (~10%)," color coded gray, or 5) "Unknown (or ~50%)," color coded black. Again, notice that the 50 percent option is marked unknown. This is because a 50 percent probability does not assert something one way or the other. A decision maker may as well not even have an assessment. If the analyst asserts a 50 percent probability, then he is actually asserting that he does not know. The analyst need only be 70 percent confident of his answers. Each analyst is trained to understand the difference between the probabilities he identifies in his answers and his level of confidence in selecting an answer. Analysts are instructed to answer every question with a 70 percent level of confidence. When a 70 percent level of confidence is applied to a 70 percent probability, the probability assessment remains at 70 percent, which is the level that a prominent decision maker (Colin Powell) requested and thus the level that analysts alert decision makers in this warning system. Again, Seventy percent was chosen based on Secretary of State Colin Powell's remarks on warning, "what I need to do is operate when the probability of something happening is about, not .2, but about .7. I can't wait until it's .99 because by then it's too late."[21]

The analyst must have supporting evidence for his answer to each question. Hyperlinks to the evidence/raw intelligence reports are listed under the evidence column in the *Indicator Key Question, Answers, & Evidence Log*, as already shown in figure 1.6 (*Indicator Key Questions, Answers, & Evidence Log*). A large quantity of reports can add weight to an answer. For instance, if an analyst has ten reports that each state a different terrorist has traveled into a given target country, and the reports are each judged "Probably Valid (~70%)," then the analyst can answer a question on terrorist travel with the assertion that a terrorist "Almost Certainly (~90%)," traveled into the target country. Thus multiple reports of 70 percent probability can amount to an assessment of 90 percent probability. The questions for which analysts lack evidence or have evidence of unknown Information Validity (about 50 percent probability that the information is valid) are answered "Unknown (or ~50%)," and are *Intelligence Gaps* (color coded black), which automatically appear in each appropriate *Indicator, Target,* and *Country Warning Narrative: What We Know, Think, & Need to Know*, which are discussed in tasks 19, 20, and 21.

An overarching theme throughout this methodology is to "get rid of the black" or get answers to Intelligence Gaps. Most hypothesis matrices will open up with many indicators at black/unknown because it only takes one report of about 50 percent validity or more to cause the computer program to open up a new hypothesis matrix. The analyst's job is to get the questions that are answered, "Unknown (or ~50%)" to a high (about 70 percent or greater) or low (about 30 or less) answer, whichever is true. He should submit Collection Requests until he can answer an indicator question at a high or low probability.

After an analyst has completed the question set for a given indicator, the computer program shows the analyst the average of his answers to the Priority 1 questions, the average to the Priority 2 questions, the average to the Priority 3 questions, and finally, a *Proposed Indicator Activity Level*, as already shown in figure 1.6 (*Indicator Key Questions, Answers, & Evidence Log*). The questions to which the analyst answered "Unknown (or ~50%)" (due either to lack of information or to unknown/50 percent probability of Information Validity) are factored into the averages as 50 percent. The analyst is given the option to accept or reject the Proposed Indicator Activity Level. If the analyst rejects the proposed level, he must provide justification by creating and prioritizing a new question or questions that address the factor(s) he thinks are missing in the question set to appropriately assess the indicator, and he must attach evidence to support his answer to the new question(s). Analysts can also determine if the question set is missing any key elements by determining if all the evidence (raw intelligence reports) shown under the indicator in the hypothesis matrix has been accounted for. The question sets help inexperienced analysts gain the understanding of experienced analysts more quickly and efficiently, which can be critical for military intelligence analysts, who frequently change assignments.

Once the analyst has settled on an *Official Indicator Activity Level* with the question set, the computer automatically displays his color-coded answer in the corresponding hypothesis matrix under the column marked "Indicator Activity Level," as shown in figure 1.8 [Hypothesis Matrix: Indicator List View (with Methodology Markings)].

The fact that these intuitive assessments (on *Indicator Activity Level*) are limited to the information in just 1 key question at a time helps guard against the intuitive pitfall that "people have difficulty keeping more than seven or so 'chunks' of information in mind at once."[22] Furthermore, the fact that these intuitive Indicator Activity Level assessments are checked by a chain of evidence in a question set and a computer calculation helps guard against an analyst's "serious random [intuitive] inconsistencies" due to his personal fatigue, and boredom, and bias.[23]

When analysts assess the information in the Anti-Indicators, they must also reassess its Priority. Anti-Indicators are set to a default of Priority 1, but if analysts believe the information is highly credible and significant enough to refute the entire hypothesis, then the analyst changes the Priority to Trump. That triggers the computer program to deactivate the target hypothesis matrix. The target still appears on the target list, but the computer program identifies it as having been discounted due to highly credible information.

2) Determine Indicator Activity Level for Quantitative Indicators Via Utility Matrix 2

Analysts use a different method to determine the Indicator Activity Level for the *quantitative* indicators, which relate to information that can be counted. For instance, analysts can count the number of unresolved cases of surveillance at a facility over a given period of time. For these indicators, the analyst simply determines 4 numerical values:

1.   The mode (typical, not average) number of unresolved suspicious incidents within 1 month in the indicator at the potential target, represented by "M" in figure 1.8 [Hypothesis Matrix: Indicator List View (with Methodology Markings)] and figure 1.9 (Utility Matrix 2). "M" is of interest because it enables analysts to recognize when a location's number of unresolved suspicious incident reports varies from its norm. "M" also enables analysts to make a fair comparison of the number of unresolved suspicious incidents between potential targets that have different capabilities and tendencies to recognize and collect on suspicious activity around them. For instance, in Saudi Arabia, a U.S. military facility has security forces at every corner of the perimeter calling counterintelligence every time someone looks at them funny, particularly every three months, when there is a new rotation of troops, because they are extremely vigilant at the beginning of their tour. However, the U.S. Embassy is much more conservative in its suspicious incident reporting.[24] Thus a U.S. military facility has a different capability and tendency to collect on suspicious activity than the U.S. Embassy. Analysts can still make a fair comparison of both locations' suspicious activity reporting by tracking each location's normal monthly level ("M") and then comparing variations from the norms.

2.   The total number of unresolved suspicious incidents within the last 3 months in the indicator at the potential target, represented by little "t" in figure 1.8 [Hypothesis Matrix: Indicator List View (with Methodology Markings)] and figure 1.9 (Utility Matrix 2). Little "t" is of interest because there is likely to be a surge of activity just before a terrorist attack.

3.   The total number of unresolved suspicious incidents over all recorded time in the indicator at the potential target represented by big "T" in figure 1.8 (Hypothesis Matrix: Indicator List View (with Methodology Markings)] and figure 1.9 (Utility Matrix 2). Big "T" is of interest because terrorists plan attacks over several years.

4.   The number of years the suspicious incident reporting dates back at the potential target, represented by "Y" in figure 1.8 [Hypothesis Matrix: Indicator List View (with Methodology Markings)] and figure 1.9 (Utility Matrix 2). "Y" is of interest because it identifies how many years big "T" spans.

Analysts enter the values of "M," "t," "T," and "Y" under the appropriate indicators of the hypothesis matrix, as shown in figure 1.8 [Hypothesis Matrix: Indicator List View (with Methodology Markings)], and the computer program calculates the Indicator Activity Level according to Utility Matrix 2 shown in figure 1.9.

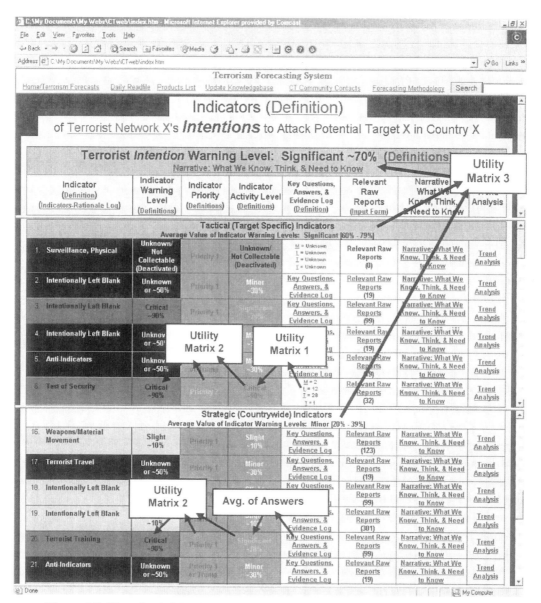

Figure 1.8. Hypothesis Matrix: Indicator List View (with Methodology Markings)

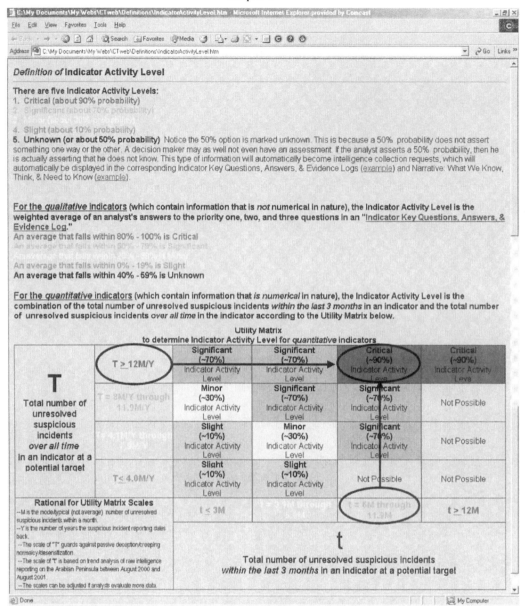

Figure 1.9. Utility Matrix 2

This is how Utility Matrix 1 works. The computer determines: Is the value of little "t" about what is expected over a 3-month timeframe, 3 times the norm (3M)? Has the value of little "t" increased by a factor of 4 (4 times 3M, or 12M)? Or has it increased by a factor somewhere in-between? The factor 4 was chosen for the high-end scale of little "t" based on case study analysis and trend analysis of suspicious incident reporting on the Arabian Peninsula from August 2000 to August 2001.[25] That is a limited data sample, so the high-end scale of little "t" should be re-evaluated as analysts obtain more data.

Similarly the computer also determines if the value of big "T" is at a small factor of the norm (such as 4M/Y) or a large factor of the norm (such as 12M/Y). The range selected for the degree of variation in big "T" is designed to guard against passive deception/creeping nor-malcy/desensitization—when an adversary repeats a threatening activity so often that it no longer appears significant. Thus, big "T" would flag a consistent number of suspicious incidents over 12 months as at least a "Significant (~70%)" Indicator Activity Level.

Finally, the computer determines, for example *if* little "t" is equal to a value between 6M and 11.9M, *and if* big "T" is equal to a value greater than or equal to 12M/Y, *then* the Indicator Activity Level is "Critical (~90%)." Then the computer displays that value in the hypothesis matrix under the column marked Indicator Activity Level, as already shown in figure 1.8 [Hypothesis Matrix: Indicator List View (with Methodology Markings)].

Determine If Miscellaneous Indicators Contain Information That Warrants a New Indicator

Analysts review the information in the Miscellaneous Indicators to determine if any new indicators should be established. This guards against analysts accidentally neglecting pertinent information that does not fit into any of the existing indicators. If an analyst believes information in a Miscellaneous Indicator warrants a new indicator, he submits a proposal to create a new indicator. If other terrorism experts approve the new indicator, then the analyst assesses its Indicator Activity Level as described above. The questions shown in the Miscellaneous Indicator Key Questions, Answers, & Evidence Log (figure 1.10) assist analysts in determining if a new indicator is warranted and also help them justify their opinion for the new indicator proposal. Analysts do not determine an Indicator Activity Level for the Miscellaneous Indicators. The Miscellaneous Indicators are color coded dark gray or "grayed out" on the indicator list view of the website display.

Deactivate Noncollectable Indicators

In some cases, the Indicator Specialist is unlikely to obtain enough information to determine an Indicator Activity Level. Notice the indicator in figure 1.5 [Hypothesis Matrix: Indicator List View (with Link to Raw Reports Display)] that is blacked out and marked "Unknown/Not Collectable (Deactivated)." If an analyst determines that the U.S. cannot or is unlikely to collect on an indicator at a given location, the analyst "deactivates" the indicator. An indicator must be collectable. The indicators listed in table 1.4 (Terrorism Indicators) are within U.S. collection capabilities; however, there are certain locations for which the U.S. cannot or is unlikely to collect on certain indicators. For instance, it would be difficult to detect surveillance of a building on an open public street in a metropolitan area, such as the World Trade Center, prior to the February 26, 1993 terrorist bombing. Thus, a methodology for analyzing indicators must enable analysts to deactivate indicators, so that the absence of information in a noncollectable indicator does not unduly lower the overall warning level assessment of a location. An indicator can be reactivated at any time. Do not confuse the option to deactivate an indicator with prioritization of an indicator. Deactivation occurs when an analyst knows or assesses that it is highly unlikely information can be *collected* at a given location, while prioritization reflects the likelihood that an activity will *take place* before an attack.

Notice an indicator can be unknown for one of three reasons: 1) information is not available because the indicator is not collectable, 2) information is not available because it has not been collected but probably can be collected, or 3) the available information is of unknown validity (about 50 percent probability of Information Validity). The first type of unknown information is treated differently than the other two types when developing assessments. Only the indicators that are unknown because they are not collectable (deactivated) are discounted from assessments. The indicators that are unknown for the other two reasons are factored into assessment averages as a 50 percent probability, and they are automatically turned into Collection Requests, which are displayed in both the *Indicator Key Questions, Answers, & Evidence Logs* and the appropriate *Indicator, Target, or Country Warning Narrative: What We Know, Think, & Need to Know,* (as explained in tasks 19, 20, and 21 of the methodology).

C:\My Documents\My Webs\CTweb\WarningPictures\"CountryTemplates\TerroristNetworkX\TargetX\KeyQu... Microsoft Internet Explorer p

File Edit View Favorites Tools Help

Address C:\My Documents\My Webs\CTweb\WarningPictures\"CountryTemplates\TerroristNetworkX\TargetX\KeyQuestionsAnswersEvidenceMiscIndicator.htm

Indicator Key Questions, Answers, & Evidence Log (Definition)
for Miscellaneous Terrorist Intentions Indicator
Target X (Imagery), Country X (Map), Terrorist Network X

All questions answered with a 70% level of confidence (reason).

#	Priority	Question (Indicator Key Questions-Rationale Log)	Almost Certainly ~90%	Probably 70%	Probably Not	Almost Certainly Not 10%	Unknown or ~50%	Evidence/ Raw Intelligence Reports
1.	NA	Does any information in this Miscellaneous Indicator warrant creating a new indicator? Answer the following questions to help make that determination.						
2.	NA	Are you sure this information does *not* fit into any of the existing Terrorism Indicators? If it does, please change the profile of this raw intelligence report in the database, so the report will appear under the appropriate indicator.	X				■	
3.	NA	Does this information addresses what must happen and what is likely to happen before a terrorist attack? File this kind of information under the evidence column for this question.	■	X			■	Relevant Raw Reports (32)
4.	NA	Are you sure this is *not* information that merely suggests a non-threatening explanation? This type of information is a "false signal," which an adversary sometimes produces as part of a Passive Deception campaign. Consider the following to help make your determination. North Korea produced signals to suggest a non-threatening explanation in 1950 by announcing false peace initiatives while mobilizing its military under the pretense of an exercise. North Korea has also used the tactic of repeating threatening signals to make them appear less significant by mobilizing its military many times for exercises. This tactic of repeating threatening signals so often that they no longer appear significant is also called, creeping normalcy or desensitization. Both methods (creating false non-threatening signals and repeating threatening signals) are designed to cause analysts to ignore the threatening signals. File this kind of information under the evidence column for this question.	X				■	Relevant Raw Reports (5)
5.	NA	Are you sure this is *not* irrelevant information that addresses activities which are unrelated to terrorist attack preparations? This type of information is "noise," which an adversary sometimes produces to surround his incrimination activity with distractions as a part of an A-type Deception campaign. Consider the following to help make your determination. Egyptian diplomats employed this type of deception by making multiple trips all over the Middle East to distract Israel from their trips to Syria. Israel knew Egypt would seek Syrian cooperation prior to an attack, but the other trips across the Middle East made the purpose of the trip to Syria appear unclear. File this kind of information under the evidence column for this question.	X				■	Relevant Raw Reports (17)
6.	1	Is this new indicator due to a change in terrorists' modus operandi? If so, describe the change under the evidence column for this question, and file the relevant raw intelligence reports there as well.	X	■			■	Relevant Raw Reports (4)
7.	1	Is this new indicator due to a change in U.S. intelligence collection capabilities? If so, describe the change under the evidence column for this question, and file the relevant raw intelligence reports there as well.	■			X	■	Relevant Raw Reports (16)
8.	1	Is this new indicator due to information analysts overlooked when creating the list of Terrorism Indicators? If so, in what other terrorist attacks (or attempted terrorist attack operations) was this indicator involved. List those attacks (or attempted attacks) under the evidence column for this question, and file the relevant raw intelligence reports there as well.	■		X		■	Relevant Raw Reports (28) Relevant terrorist attacks (or attempted attacks)

An affirmative answer to only one of the Priority 1 questions can be sufficient justification for creating a new indicator.

Based on your answers to the above questions, the methodology's computer application suggests a new indicator is:

Almost Certainly Required: X
Probably Required:
Probably Not Required:
Almost Certainly not Required:
Not Enough Information to Determine:

Reason suggestion was rejected, if applicable.

Submit an Indicator Proposal Form.

Figure 1.10. Miscellaneous Indicator Key Questions, Answers, & Evidence Log

Determine Indicator Warning Level Via Utility Matrix 2

So now the analysts have an Indicator Activity Level for each of the 68 Terrorism Indicators via the *Indicator Key Questions, Answers, & Evidence Log* or *Utility Matrix 1*, but that is not the final answer on an indicator because some indicators are more significant than others (as explained in task 2). The computer application automatically factors the Indicator Priority into the next assessment level.

In fact, from here on, all the warning level calculations are automated. The third group of analysts, *Senior Warning Officers*, is responsible for monitoring and approving all the warning levels that the computer application automatically produces and updates on the webpages. Whenever a Senior Warning Officer rejects a warning level that the system produces, he is required to write a justification in the appropriate *Indicator, Target, or Country Warning Narrative: What We Know, Think, & Need to Know*, which is described later in tasks 19, 20, and 21. Automating these warning level calculations ensures accuracy in calculations, immediate updates, consistency in the necessary, recurring judgments, and saves time and manpower.

Anyway, the computer application combines the Indicator Activity Level and the Indicator Priority to determine an *Indicator Warning Level* [on a 5-level scale of 1) *Critical (~90%)*, about 90 percent probability, color coded red on the website, 2) *Significant (~70%)*, color coded orange, 3) *Minor (~30%)*, color coded yellow, 4) *Slight (~10%)*, color coded gray, and 5) *Unknown (or ~50%)*, color coded black] according to Utility Matrix 3 shown in figure 1.11. For instance, if the designated Counterterrorism Community expert on weapons movement had assessed the *Terrorist Training Indicator* as "Significant (~70%)," then since that is a Priority 1 indicator, its Indicator Warning Level would be "Critical (~90%)." The resulting value is displayed in the hypothesis matrix under the column marked Indicator Warning Level, as already shown in figure 1.8 [Hypothesis Matrix: Indicator List View (with Methodology Markings)].

Also notice the utility matrix causes an indicator assessed at a "Minor (~30%)" Indicator Activity Level, which would not have been given much attention, to be raised to an Intelligence Gap ("Unknown (or ~50%)" Indicator Warning Level) and turned into a Collection Request if the information relates to a Priority 1 indicator, such as a high damage capacity nuclear capability indicator. This is because, in matters of security, it is best to err on the side of caution; so when the information relates to such a significant threat, it is best to make the effort to make certain that the threat does not exist rather than accepting without question that the threat is a minor probability. When an indicator is "bumped up" to an Intelligence Gap, all the key questions on the indicator (shown in the Indicator Key Questions Answers and Evidence Log (figure 1.6)) are displayed as Collection Requests in the appropriate *Indicator, Target, or Country Warning Narrative: What We Know, Think, & Need to Know*, (as explained in tasks 19, 20, and 21 of the methodology).

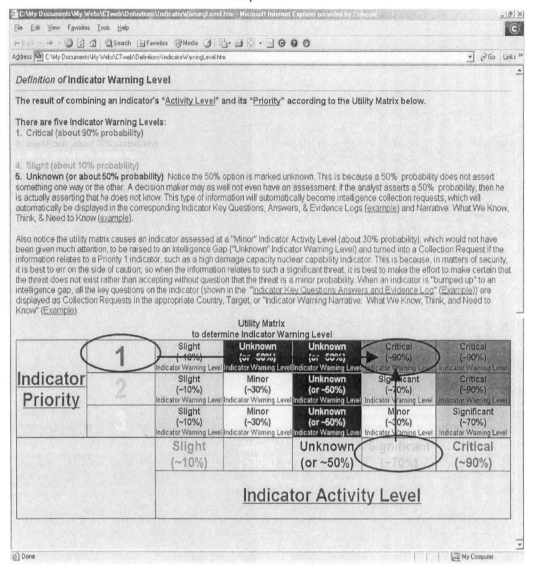

Figure 1.11. Utility Matrix 3

Task 11: Assess *Terrorist Intention Warning Level* (Daily)

Now that analysts have assessed an Indicator Warning Level for each of the 68 indicators of terrorist intentions, terrorist capability, and target vulnerability (the 3 components of risk), the computer can calculate a warning level for each of those 3 components. The computer calculates the *Terrorist Intention Warning Level* for a target [on a 5-level scale of 1) *Critical (~90%)*, about 90 percent probability, color coded red on the website, 2) *Significant (~70%)*, color coded orange, 3) *Minor (~30%)*, color coded yellow, 4) *Slight (~10%)*, color coded gray, and 5) *Unknown (or ~50%)*, color coded black] by:

1. Averaging all the Indicator Warning Levels for the active tactical (target-specific) Terror-ist Intention Indicators,

2. Averaging all the Indicator Warning Levels for the active strategic (countrywide) Terrorist Intention Indicators, and then

3. Combining the 2 averaged values according to Utility Matrix 4 shown in figure 1.12.

For instance, if the average of the tactical indicators was "Significant (~70%)," and the average of the strategic indicators was "Minor (~30%)," then the overall Terrorist Intention Warning Level would be "Significant (~70%)." Miscellaneous Indicators and deactivated indicators are not factored into the averages.

Given the reality that intelligence information is never absolute, this methodology never allows a risk factor to be assessed as nonexistent. Therefore, "Slight (~10%)" is the smallest value a risk factor can be, and the smallest value risk can be.

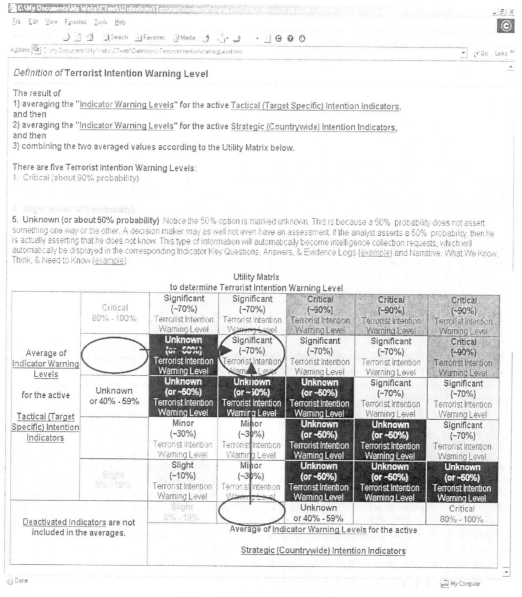

Figure 1.12. Utility Matrix 4

The resulting value is displayed at the top of the terrorist intentions indicator list webpage, under the heading marked "Terrorist Intention Warning Level," as already shown in figure 1.8 [Hypothesis Matrix: Indicator List View (with Methodology Markings)]. Thus, figure 1.8 shows the assessment that Terrorist Network X's intention to attack Target X in Country X is "Significant (~70%)."

The Terrorist Intention Warning Level is also displayed on the target list webpage, as shown for Target A in Country X in figure 1.13 (Hypothesis Matrix: Target List View).

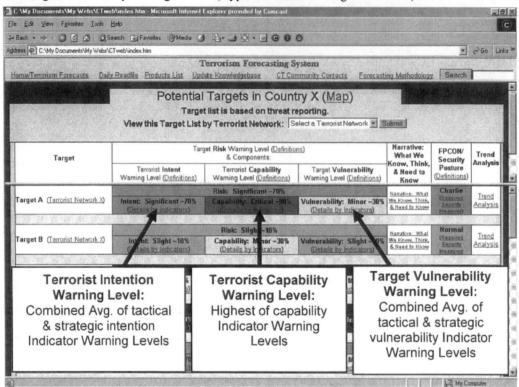

Figure 1.13. Hypothesis Matrix: Target List View

Task 12: Assess *Terrorist Capability Warning Level* (Daily)

The computer determines the *Terrorist Capability Warning Level* for a given country [on a 5-level scale of 1) *Critical (~90%)*, about 90 percent probability, color coded red on the website, 2) *Significant (~70%)*, color coded orange, 3) *Minor (~30%)*, color coded yellow, 4) *Slight (~10%)*, color coded gray, and 5) *Unknown (or ~50%)*, color coded black] by taking the highest of all the Indicator Warning Levels for the active terrorist capability, *lethal agent/technique* indicators. The *delivery method* Indicator Warning Levels are not used because it is primarily the lethal agent/technique, rather than the delivery method, that determines the level of damage that can be inflicted. The Miscellaneous Indicators and deactivated indicators are also excluded. Taking the highest value is more rational than taking an average value because a group's most dangerous capability (such as biological) is not reduced by other lower capabilities (such as conventional bombing). Whereas with the Terrorist Intention Indicators, taking an average makes sense because if terrorists have not yet completed an activity that must take place before an attack, then their attack plan is probably not yet viable.

The resulting Terrorist Capability Warning Level value is displayed at the top of the terrorist capability indicator list webpage (like the terrorist intention indicator list webpage already shown in figure 1.8), under a heading marked "Terrorist Capability Warning Level." Thus, the terrorist capability indicator list webpage would show the assessment that a terrorist network's capability to attack in a given country is Critical (~90%) about 90 percent probability, Significant (~70%), Minor (~30%), Slight (~10%), or Unknown (or ~50%).

The Terrorist Capability Warning Level is also displayed on the target list webpage, as already shown for Target A in Country X in figure 1.13 (Hypothesis Matrix: Target List View).

Task 13: Assess *Target Vulnerability Warning Level* (Daily)

The computer program calculates a target's *Vulnerability Warning Level* [on a 5-level scale of 1) *Critical (~90%)*, about 90 percent probability, color coded red on the website, 2) *Significant (~70%)*, color coded orange, 3) *Minor (~30%)*, color coded yellow, 4) *Slight (~10%)*, color coded gray, and 5) *Unknown (or ~50%)*, color coded black] the same way as was done for the Terrorist Intention Warning Level, by:

1. Averaging all the Indicator Warning Levels in the list of active tactical (target-specific) vulnerability indicators,

2. Averaging all the Indicator Warning Levels in the list of active strategic (countrywide) vulnerability indicators, and then

3. Combining the 2 averaged values according to a Utility Matrix like the one already shown in figure 1.12 (Utility Matrix 4).

Taking an average value is rational for the vulnerability indicators because none of the factors that affect vulnerability can negate the effects of the others. Again, the Miscellaneous Indicators and deactivated indicators are not factored into the averages.

The resulting Target Vulnerability Warning Level value is displayed at the top of the vulnerability indicator list webpage (like the terrorist intention indicator list webpage already shown in figure 1.8), under a heading marked "Target Vulnerability Warning Level." Thus, the vulnerability indicator list webpage might show the assessment that Target X's vulnerability to a terrorist attack is "Minor (~30%)."

The Target Vulnerability Warning Level is also displayed on the target list webpage, as already shown for Target A in Country X in figure 1.13 (Hypothesis Matrix: Target List View).

Task 14: Assess *Target Risk Warning Level* (Daily)

Now that analysts have a warning level for each of the 3 components of risk (terrorist intentions, terrorist capability, and target vulnerability), the computer can calculate a risk warning level for a given target. The computer program calculates the *Target Risk Warning Level* [on a 5-level scale of 1) *Critical (~90%)*, about 90 percent probability, color coded red on the website, 2) *Significant (~70%)*, color coded orange, 3) *Minor (~30%)*, color coded yellow, 4) *Slight (~10%)*, color coded gray, and 5) *Unknown (or ~50%)*, color coded black] by averaging the Terrorist Intention, Terrorist Capability, and Target Vulnerability Warning Levels. Averaging is rational because it would not allow a single risk factor with a zero value to produce a zero risk value for a target. In an ideal world, if a risk factor does not exist, then risk does not exist. However, in the real world, intelligence information is never absolute, therefore, this methodology purposefully excludes the possibility of either a risk factor or risk being assessed as nonexistent. The Target Risk Warning Level is displayed on the target list webpage above the Terrorist Intention, Terrorist Capability, and Target Vulnerability Warning Levels, as already shown for Target A in Country X in figure 1.13 (Hypothesis Matrix: Target List View).

Task 15: Assess *Country Risk Warning Level* (Daily)

Now that analysts have a risk warning level for each reported target in a country, the computer can calculate an overall risk warning level for the country. The computer program determines the *Country Risk Warning Level* by taking the highest Target Risk Warning Level in the country. Taking the highest value is rational because, in matters of security, it is best to be aware of the worst possibilities. The Country Risk Warning Level is displayed on the country list webpage, as shown in figure 1.14 (Hypothesis Matrix: Country List View).

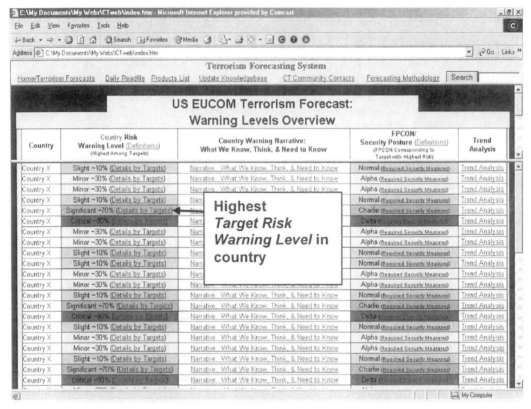

Figure 1.14. Hypothesis Matrix: Country List View

The definitions of those Country Risk Warning Levels are shown on the Country Risk Warning Level definition webpage (shown in figure 1.15), which is hyperlinked to the country list view webpage (already shown in figure 1.14).

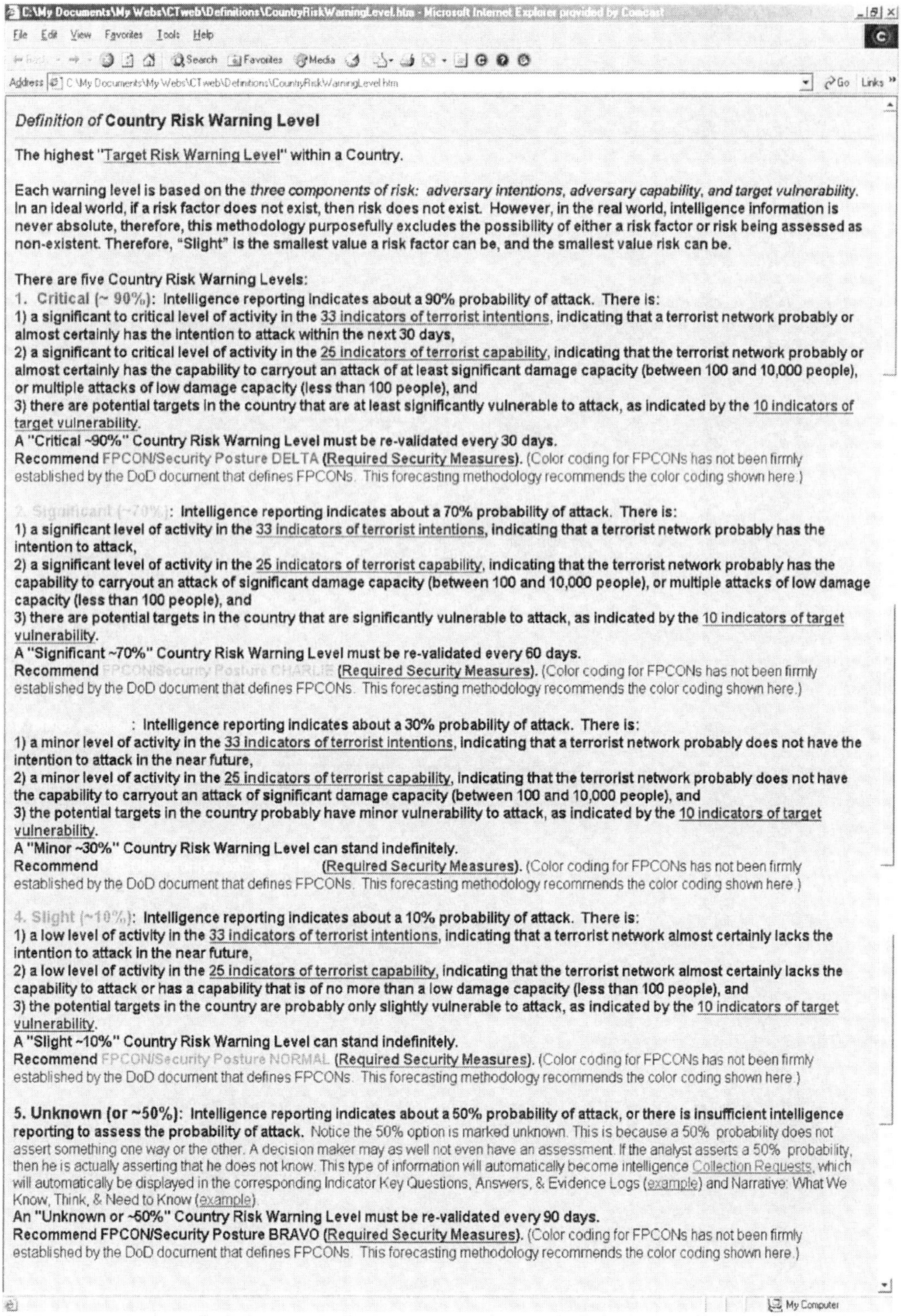

C:\My Documents\My Webs\CTweb\Definitions\CountryRiskWarningLevel.htm - Microsoft Internet Explorer provided by Comcast

File Edit View Favorites Tools Help

Address C:\My Documents\My Webs\CTweb\Definitions\CountryRiskWarningLevel.htm

Definition of **Country Risk Warning Level**

The highest "Target Risk Warning Level" within a Country.

Each warning level is based on the *three components of risk: adversary intentions, adversary capability, and target vulnerability.* In an ideal world, if a risk factor does not exist, then risk does not exist. However, in the real world, intelligence information is never absolute, therefore, this methodology purposefully excludes the possibility of either a risk factor or risk being assessed as non-existent. Therefore, "Slight" is the smallest value a risk factor can be, and the smallest value risk can be.

There are five Country Risk Warning Levels:

1. Critical (~ 90%): Intelligence reporting indicates about a 90% probability of attack. There is:
1) a significant to critical level of activity in the 33 indicators of terrorist intentions, indicating that a terrorist network probably or almost certainly has the intention to attack within the next 30 days,
2) a significant to critical level of activity in the 25 indicators of terrorist capability, indicating that the terrorist network probably or almost certainly has the capability to carryout an attack of at least significant damage capacity (between 100 and 10,000 people), or multiple attacks of low damage capacity (less than 100 people), and
3) there are potential targets in the country that are at least significantly vulnerable to attack, as indicated by the 10 indicators of target vulnerability.
A "Critical ~90%" Country Risk Warning Level must be re-validated every 30 days.
Recommend FPCON/Security Posture DELTA (Required Security Measures). (Color coding for FPCONs has not been firmly established by the DoD document that defines FPCONs. This forecasting methodology recommends the color coding shown here.)

2. Significant (~70%): Intelligence reporting indicates about a 70% probability of attack. There is:
1) a significant level of activity in the 33 indicators of terrorist intentions, indicating that a terrorist network probably has the intention to attack,
2) a significant level of activity in the 25 indicators of terrorist capability, indicating that the terrorist network probably has the capability to carryout an attack of significant damage capacity (between 100 and 10,000 people), or multiple attacks of low damage capacity (less than 100 people), and
3) there are potential targets in the country that are significantly vulnerable to attack, as indicated by the 10 indicators of target vulnerability.
A "Significant ~70%" Country Risk Warning Level must be re-validated every 60 days.
Recommend FPCON/Security Posture CHARLIE (Required Security Measures). (Color coding for FPCONs has not been firmly established by the DoD document that defines FPCONs. This forecasting methodology recommends the color coding shown here.)

: Intelligence reporting indicates about a 30% probability of attack. There is:
1) a minor level of activity in the 33 indicators of terrorist intentions, indicating that a terrorist network probably does not have the intention to attack in the near future,
2) a minor level of activity in the 25 indicators of terrorist capability, indicating that the terrorist network probably does not have the capability to carryout an attack of significant damage capacity (between 100 and 10,000 people), and
3) the potential targets in the country probably have minor vulnerability to attack, as indicated by the 10 indicators of target vulnerability.
A "Minor ~30%" Country Risk Warning Level can stand indefinitely.
Recommend (Required Security Measures). (Color coding for FPCONs has not been firmly established by the DoD document that defines FPCONs. This forecasting methodology recommends the color coding shown here.)

4. Slight (~10%): Intelligence reporting indicates about a 10% probability of attack. There is:
1) a low level of activity in the 33 indicators of terrorist intentions, indicating that a terrorist network almost certainly lacks the intention to attack in the near future,
2) a low level of activity in the 25 indicators of terrorist capability, indicating that the terrorist network almost certainly lacks the capability to attack or has a capability that is of no more than a low damage capacity (less than 100 people), and
3) the potential targets in the country are probably only slightly vulnerable to attack, as indicated by the 10 indicators of target vulnerability.
A "Slight ~10%" Country Risk Warning Level can stand indefinitely.
Recommend FPCON/Security Posture NORMAL (Required Security Measures). (Color coding for FPCONs has not been firmly established by the DoD document that defines FPCONs. This forecasting methodology recommends the color coding shown here.)

5. Unknown (or ~50%): Intelligence reporting indicates about a 50% probability of attack, or there is insufficient intelligence reporting to assess the probability of attack. Notice the 50% option is marked unknown. This is because a 50% probability does not assert something one way or the other. A decision maker may as well not even have an assessment. If the analyst asserts a 50% probability, then he is actually asserting that he does not know. This type of information will automatically become intelligence Collection Requests, which will automatically be displayed in the corresponding Indicator Key Questions, Answers, & Evidence Logs (example) and Narrative: What We Know, Think, & Need to Know (example).
An "Unknown or ~50%" Country Risk Warning Level must be re-validated every 90 days.
Recommend FPCON/Security Posture BRAVO (Required Security Measures). (Color coding for FPCONs has not been firmly established by the DoD document that defines FPCONs. This forecasting methodology recommends the color coding shown here.)

My Computer

Figure 1.15. Country Risk Warning Level Definition Webpage

Task 16: Update/Study Trend Analysis of Indicator Warning Levels (Monthly)

This explanation has now shown how the methodology determines various warning levels, and that they are displayed in 3 primary views: indicator list, target list, and country list. There is also trend analysis for each view. Figure 1.8 (Hypothesis Matrix: Indicator List View), already shown in task 10, shows what a given indicator looks like today. Figure 1.16 (Trend Analysis of Indicator X) shows what the indicator looked like in January of 2002, February of 2002, March of 2002 and so on.

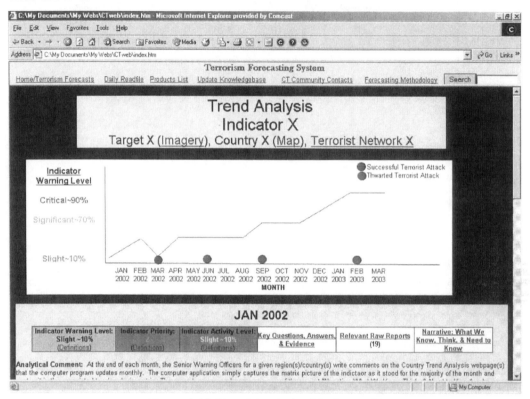

Figure 1.16. Trend Analysis of Indicator X

The computer automatically captures the Indicator Warning Level at the end of each month and plots it on the graph. The computer captures the level as it stood for the majority of the month. The computer also saves a copy of the current *Indicator Warning Narrative: What We Know, Think, & Need to Know*, and the *Indicator Key Questions, Answers, & Evidence Log*. Senior Warning Officers write analytical comments. The comment includes a discussion of successful and thwarted terrorist operations so analysts and decision makers can recognize successes and failures in the system. The database temples for trend analysis remind analysts that successful terrorist attacks are not the only source of useful reference events; thwarted terrorist attacks also provide useful reference evidence because the terrorists still carried out their preparations for the attack despite the fact that it did not take place. Trend analysis helps analysts recognize patterns and anomalies, which can in turn be used to adjust the scales for determining warning levels in the methodology. "Experience Is Inevitable, Learning Is Not," according to researchers, who explain that people must actively pursue a systematic way to gain feedback on their system.

Task 17: Update/Study Trend Analysis of Target Risk Warning Levels (Monthly)

A target-oriented trend analysis is also maintained. Figure 1.13 (Hypothesis Matrix: Target List View), already shown in task 11, shows what Target X looks like today. Figure 1.17 (Trend Analysis of Target X) shows what Target X looked like in January 2002, February 2002, March 2002 and so on. Again, the computer automatically captures the warning level at the end of each month and plots it on the graph. Again, Senior Warning Officers write a comment discussing warning failures and successes and how the methodology will be adjusted, if necessary.

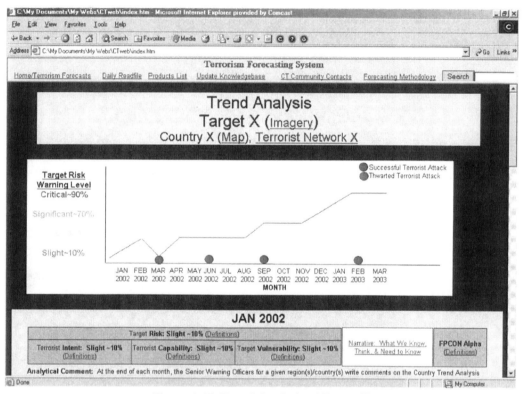

Figure 1.17. Trend Analysis of Target X

Task 18: Update/Study Trend Analysis of Country Risk Warning Levels (Monthly)

Finally, a country-oriented trend analysis is maintained. Figure 1.14 (Hypothesis Matrix: Country List View), already shown in task 15, shows what Country X looks like today. Figure 1.18 (Trend Analysis of Country X) shows what Country X looked like at points in the past. Again, the computer automatically captures the warning level at the end of each month and plots it on the graph. Again, Senior Warning Officers write a comment discussing warning failures and successes and how the methodology will be adjusted, if necessary. Although this trend analysis may appear to involve an unusually high amount of low-level work for a senior-level analyst, it is necessary in order to truly develop his understanding of the big picture.

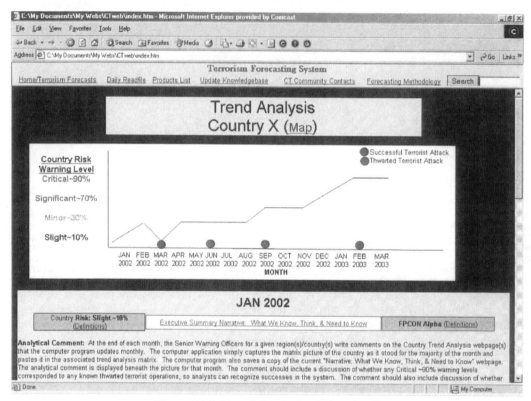

Figure 1.18. Trend Analysis of Country X

Phase V: Focus Collectors on Intelligence Gaps to Refine/Update Conclusions (Using Narratives that Describe What We Know, Think, and Need to Know)

Task 19: Write/Update *Indicator Warning Narrative: What We Know, Think, & Need to Know* (Daily)

Thus far, the methodology has provided color-coded graphic representations of warning assessments, but of course narratives are necessary to explain the details behind each color-coded warning level. Narratives are provided for each of the 3 graphic views—indicators, targets, and countries.

After an Indicator Specialist has updated his *Indicator Key Questions, Answers, & Evidence Log* with the new raw reporting of the day, he also updates his *Indicator Warning Narrative: What We Know, Think, & Need to Know*. The key question set provides an outline of all the major points that the narrative should address. The narrative begins with a description of what the analyst knows and thinks about the indicator, then is followed by a set of bullets on what he doesn't know—Intelligence Gaps stated as questions for intelligence collectors. The questions to which an analyst answered "Unknown (or ~50%)" in the *Indicator Key Questions, Answers, & Evidence Log* automatically appear as *Collection Requests* in the narrative. Analysts can add additional Collection Requests if necessary. Analysts follow 4 key principles when generating Collection Requests:

1. Collection Requests must be stated as questions for intelligence collectors.

2. The questions can be as specific as necessary—such as, "Where is the man in the attached photograph?"

3. Collection Requests should be generated for every indicator to guard against the warning pitfall of "seeking evidence to confirm a favorite hypothesis."

4. Collection Requests should be geared toward disproving (rather than proving) a hypothesis.

This method of including Collection Requests in online finished assessments, updated daily and broken out by indicator, target, and country, helps focus intelligence collection in an efficient and timely way that supports warning. The U.S. Defense Indications and Warning System (DIWS) states that indicators should be turned into collection plans in order to focus collection in a way that will support warning.[26] Thus, the list of prioritized Terrorism Indicators and corresponding question sets in the *Indicator Key Question, Answers, & Evidence Logs* should be the prioritized focus of intelligence collection to effectively support terrorism warning.

Furthermore, the nature of warning demands timely assessment and response. Before the September 11, 2001 terrorist attacks, there was just 1 month between the Priority 1 indication of terrorist travel and the attack.[27] Today, assessments can take a month to get published and disseminated, and they are outdated soon thereafter. By placing the Collection Requests in near-real-time finished assessments online where collectors and analysts can work from the same near-real-time waning picture, the intelligence cycle of collection feeding analysis and analysis feeding collection is timelier. Another advantage of including Intelligence Gaps in finished assessments is that it guards against analysts overstating the certainty of their assessments (high or low).

Task 20: Write/Update Executive Summary for *Target Warning Narrative: What We Know, Think, & Need to Know* (Daily)

The computer program combines all the indicator narratives into a potential target narrative. Senior Warning Officers write and maintain executive summaries for each potential target narrative. They determine if they concur with the warning levels that their partly automated methodology produced with the hypothesis and utility matrix logic. This is a reality check of the warning levels that will be published in the webpages. If the Senior Warning Officers do not concur with any of the warning levels that their partly automated methodology produced, they must write an explanation of why they have overridden the system. Senior Warning Officers can add Collection Requests if the consolidated picture of indicator assessments on a specific target reveals any additional gaps in intelligence. The template for a *Target Warning Narrative: What We Know, Think, & Need to Know* is shown in figure 1.19. The Indicator Warning Levels are also displayed in this narrative and include hyperlinks that bookmark to the paragraph on the corresponding indicator in the document. *These narratives are ready to print with the latest daily updates at any time for decision makers.*

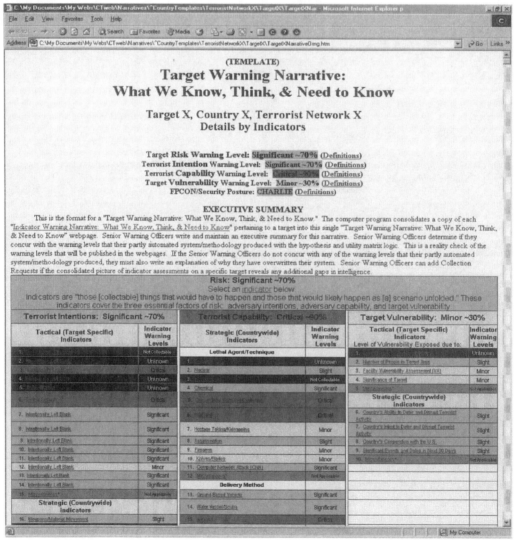

Figure 1.19. Template *Target Warning Narrative: What We Know, Think, & Need to Know*

Task 21: Write/Update Executive Summary for *Country Warning Narrative: What We Know, Think, & Need to Know* (Daily)

Finally, the computer program combines all the potential target executive summaries into a country narrative. Again, Senior Warning Officers are also responsible for maintaining executive summaries for the country narratives and justifying any overwrites they make to the warning levels that their partly automated methodology produced with the hypothesis and utility matrix logic. Again, Senior Warning Officers can add Collection Requests if the consolidated picture of specific target assessments within a country reveals any additional gaps in intelligence.

Phase VI: Communicate Conclusions/Give Warning (Using Website Templates)

Task 22: Brief Decision Maker with Website Templates (As Required)

The final task of a warning system is to convey the warning. Senior Warning Officers brief the warning levels to a decision maker using the website templates. The number one cause of warning failure is decision makers ignoring intelligence, which may also be characterized as analysts failing to persuade decision makers. In the Intelligence Community, it is common for a junior analyst to brief a decision maker who has many more years of experience on the subject. Thus, an analyst who attempts to rely on his intuitive experience rather than demonstrating a reasoning process is unlikely to fare well against the decision maker's more experienced intuition (justified or not). In addition, "because policy makers know that [even experienced] analysts, like most mortals, cannot foretell the future, they need, instead, to be persuaded by clear articulation of rationale and evidence. . . . Unless analysts can demonstrate why and how the likelihood of a given event is increasing . . . their words are of little use."[28] Therefore, analysts must do everything within their power to make a warning assessment/picture persuasive.

The website templates are designed to convey the structured reasoning process behind each warning level. Leading graphic interface experts have found that the most effective way to capitalize on "human perceptual skills [which] are remarkable, but largely underutilized by current graphical interfaces," is to show "overview first, [then] zoom and filter, and then details-on-demand."[29] The warning assessments/pictures in this website follow that design principle via 3 primary types of color-coded warning picture views: 1) country list view, 2) target list view, and 3) indicator list view (of terrorist intentions, terrorist capability, or target vulnerability). With the click of a button, analysts can further take decision makers all the way down to the detailed indications contained in individual raw intelligence reports shown as supporting evidence in the *Indicator Key Questions, Answers, & Evidence Logs*. Decision makers sometimes want to know these details because it can cost millions of dollars and involve difficult political negotiations with a host country to increase a security posture/Force Protection Condition (FPCON). This layout also allows decision makers, who do not have the time or need to see details, a quick overview, while still providing details-on-demand.

Surprisingly though, a clear logical presentation of information is not always enough to get a decision maker to trust an analytical product, as demonstrated prior to Saddam Hussein's August 1990 invasion of Kuwait:

> Indicators were assessed early and accurately. . . . Collection was honed and focused; coordination with the analytic community was constant; and policy officials were informed of our conclusions at each major stage in the development of the threat, personally as well as in writing . . . [with] a standard warning chronology . . . tracing the development of events during the past year. . . . Nevertheless, the warning . . . was not taken seriously because U.S. officials talked with, and accepted the

judgment of a number of leaders in the Middle East as well as the Soviet Union.[30]

In this case, the *decision makers trusted the opinion of foreign leaders over their own intelligence warning system*. Therefore the question arises: What more can analysts do to gain decision makers' trust in their assessments?

Research shows that the process by which people develop trust for a product follows these steps: "Frequency [leads] to awareness, awareness to familiarity, and familiarity to trust."[31] Thus, the Intelligence Community should agree on a universal display format for intelligence warning information, and use it every time they brief a decision maker so that that repetition can lead to awareness, familiarity, and consequently trust. Furthermore, by maintaining the display format on a website, analysts will further promote frequency of use and familiarity in the product.

If a decision maker heeds an analyst's warning and alters a security posture/FPCON, the analyst enters the new corresponding value for the Security Posture/FPCON Indicator, amongst all the other vulnerability indicators. Then the computer program automatically recalculates the vulnerability and risk levels according to the new Security Posture/FPCON, and displays them as shown in figure 1.20 [Hypothesis Matrix: Target List View (with Methodology Markings)]. This enables decision makers to immediately see how their decisions affect the risk level to a given threat.

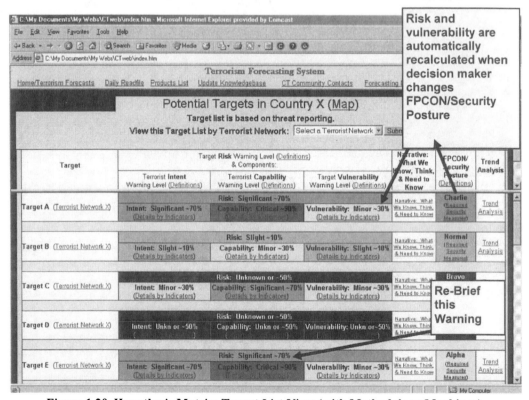

Figure 1.20. Hypothesis Matrix: Target List View (with Methodology Markings)

Task 23: Rebrief Decision Maker with New Evidence in Website Templates (As Required)

If a decision maker does not alter an FPCON after hearing the analyst's assessment, the analyst returns to the decision maker with new evidence to press the assessment until the decision maker heeds the warning. Some intelligence experts dispute that it is an analyst's responsibility to persuade decision makers in the warning process. They argue that if an analyst informs decision makers of a potential event, but decision makers reject that assessment, then that is a case of policy failure, not intelligence failure.[32] However, as a former National Intelligence Officer (NIO) for Warning explains, "We now understand that warning is a repetitive process that is not completed until national policymakers accept the threat as genuine or reject the evidence as not persuasive. . . . [W]arning must be repeated as and when more persuasive evidence is obtained."[33]

Secretary of State Colin Powell says it eloquently, "[Analysts must] recognize that more often than not, I will throw them out, saying 'na doesn't sound right, get outta here.' What I need from my I&W system at that point is, 'That old bastard, I'm going to prove him wrong.' And go back and accumulate more information, come back the next day and give me some more and get thrown out again. Constantly come back . . . and persuade me that I better start paying attention."[34] This is in line with DCI's statement that the purpose of intelligence is "not to observe and comment, but to warn and protect."[35]

The new evidence not only appears in the hypothesis matrices each day; it is also automatically listed in a *Daily Readfile* webpage as shown in figure 1.21. *All* the day's new raw intelligence reports are listed in the Daily Readfile. The reports are grouped in order of their level of Information Validity (Almost Certainly Valid (~90%), Probably Valid (~70%), Unknown Validity (or ~50%), Probably Not Valid (~30%), and 5) Almost Certainly Not Valid (~10%)), and then the reports are alphabetized by county within each of those validity groupings. This enables users to find the latest reports without burrowing down into all the hypothesis matrices and trying to remember which reports they have read and which they have not. A Daily Readfile Archives webpage (also shown in figure 1.21) enables users to easily find past daily read files and reports. *However, analysts should use the hypothesis matrices (not the Daily Readfile) when they brief a threat, so that each new report is put into context with all the other reports relating to that hypothesis/potential target.*

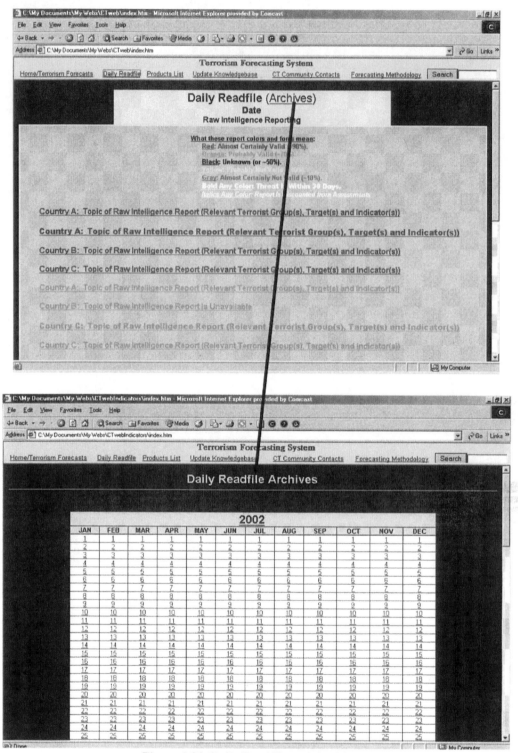

Figure 1.21. Daily Readfile and Archives

Closing Key Points

So, that's it for the explanation. Raw reports and finished assessments are all there is in intelligence production. Finished assessments can be provided in 2 primary formats: color-coded pictures for quick reference, or narratives for people who want to read detailed paragraphs. By including Collection Requests in the narratives, analysts guard against overstating their certainty on an issue and also enable intelligence collectors to find the 2 primary types of information that they need before tapping a source: 1) all the Intelligence Community knows on a given topic and 2) all that the Intelligence Community needs to know on the topic. This way, collection not only feeds analysis, but analysis also feeds collection, which is the way the intelligence cycle is supposed to work. Tasks in this methodology have been automated wherever possible to counter the time-constraint objection many analysts voice against using structured techniques. "The process takes too long," can no longer be an excuse for neglecting tested and proven analytical techniques. Furthermore, analysts function in a coordinated, systematic effort that saves time, which leads to the staffing plan necessary to operate this methodology.

Staffing Plan

Overview

A critical point to emphasize about this system is that for it to succeed, it must have a trained, coordinated staff to operate it.

> It is a sad fact that many projects, particularly those involving information systems, fail to deliver against their objectives on time and within budget. . . . One thing that stands out in the analysis of all projects, whether successful or otherwise, is that projects are about people. Few information systems projects fail for technical reasons. Most projects fail because they are not effectively managed and the most important and complex aspect of the management task is managing relationships with the people involved.[36]

Experts are so adamant about that point, that they even caution/explain, "When we design a new information system, we are redesigning the organization."[37]

Three types of analysts are required to operate this methodology: Raw Reporting Profilers, Indicator Specialists, and Senior Warning Officers. This staffing plan provides: 1) a job description for each type of analyst position and 2) an explanation of how many of each type of analyst are required for worldwide coverage—84 Raw Reporting Profilers, 18 Indicator Specialists, and 5 Senior Warning Officers. That staff, 107 analysts, is far less than the Intelligence Community currently has working to provide worldwide terrorism I&W assessments. This system is a highly efficient use of personnel because recurring, analytical tasks are automated wherever possible, and because the analysts are working in a coordinated, systematic effort. In the training progression of analysts, Raw Reporting Profilers can become Indicator Specialists, and Indicator Specialists can become Senior Warning Officers.

Raw Reporting Profilers

Job Description

Raw Reporting Profilers are a large group of junior analysts who are responsible for reading through the thousands of incoming terrorism related-raw intelligence reports in the Intelligence Community Master Database and entering them into the Terrorism Forecasting Database under the appropriate indicators, key questions, targets, countries, terrorist groups, and other data profile elements (as explained in task 6 of the methodology).

Explanation of Number Required

Eighty-four Raw Reporting Profilers are required. The author estimates that 2500 raw intelligence reports on terrorism are received daily.[38] On average, 1 person can read, profile, and enter 1 raw report into the Terrorism Forecasting Database in 10 minutes. Therefore, if a person reviews and profiles reports for 5 hours in an 8-hour working day, he can profile 30 reports daily. Thus, it would take 84 people to review and profile 2500 reports a day. Profiling 30 reports may seem like a small accomplishment for a person in a day, but this is actually a highly efficient 1-pass system that is consistent with good time-management practices. Analysts make the critical decisions on a report in their first "pass" or review of the report. No report is ever placed aside to be reviewed again later, or worse, forgotten, when analysts are first trying to identify the important information they should glean from the report. Instead analysts are forced to profile reports immediately and assisted to identify the important points as they enter/profile the reports in the Terrorism Forecasting Database according to the data profile elements identified in figure 1.4. Thus, the 30 raw intelligence reports that each of the 84 Raw Reporting Profilers profiles a day is a good accomplishment and efficient use of resources.

The number of these analysts could be reduced by using an artificial intelligence computer program to presort the 2500 reports based on key words. These programs are about 80 percent accurate according to research. Humans are also about 80 percent accurate according to research.[39] By combining both, analysts can increase accuracy and save time and manpower.

Indicator Specialists

Job Description

Indicator Specialists are the Counterterrorism Community's designated experts on a given indicator or set of indicators for a given terrorist network(s) and country(s). These specialized analysts are responsible for:

1. Updating, as necessary, the profile of the raw intelligence reports that fall under their indicators in the Terrorism Forecasting Database (as explained in task 6 of the methodology).

2. Assessing the Indicator Activity Level (as explained in task 10 of the methodology) for their indicators [on a 5-level scale of 1) Critical (~90%), about 90 percent probability, color coded red on the website, 2) Significant (~70%), color coded orange, 3) Minor (~30%), color coded yellow, 4) Slight (~10%), color coded gray, and 5) Unknown (or ~50%), color coded black] by the following process:

    1) For the *qualitative* indicators, answering question sets and matching evidence/raw intelligence reports to support their answers to those questions in the *Indicator Key*

Questions, Answers, & Evidence Log webpage(s), or

2) For the *quantitative* indicators, determining 4 numerical values: 1) the mode (typical, not average) number of unresolved suspicious incidents within 1 month in the indicator, represented by "M," 2) the total number of unresolved suspicious incidents within the last 3 months in the indicator, represented by little "t," 3) the total number of unresolved suspicious incidents over time in the indicator, represented by big "T," and 4) the number of years the suspicious incident reporting dates back, represented by "Y."

3. Adding and refining questions to the *Indicator Key Questions, Answers, & Evidence Log* webpage(s) for their indicator(s) as necessary (as explained in task 3 of the methodology).

4. Generating Collection Requests for their indicator(s) (as explained in task 19 of the methodology).

5. Writing and maintaining an *Indicator Warning Narrative: What We Know, Think, & Need to Know* webpage for each of their indicators (as explained in task 19 of the methodology).

6. Writing analytical comment inputs for Senior Warning Officers on the indicator trend analysis webpage pictures that the partly automated methodology produces monthly (as explained in task 16 of the methodology).

7. If applicable, maintaining descriptions of the terrorist group(s) and network(s) for which they are responsible (as shown on the webpage templates enclosed on the CD).

8. Determining annually with Senior Warning Officers if any new indicators need to be established (as explained in task 1 of the methodology) by:

   1) Reviewing the raw intelligence reports filed under the Miscellaneous Indicators to determine if any kinds of significant terrorist activity have been overlooked.
   2) Reviewing U.S. collection capabilities to determine if the U.S. has gained the capability to collect on any additional terrorist activities.
   3) Reviewing case studies of terrorist operations to identify changes in terrorist modus operandi and determine if terrorists are conducting any new activities against which U.S. intelligence can collect.

Explanation of Number Required

Eighteen Indicator Specialists are required, each responsible for an indicator or set of indicators for a given region or regions. When terrorism experts meet to validate the indicator list, they also ensure the indicators are divided logically among the analysts that will assess them. The 68 Terrorism Indicators are grouped under 5 types of Indicator Specialists in a way that optimizes the analysts' efficiency and ability to assess them. For instance, the analyst who tracks suspicious incident reporting would be in the best position to know how well a host nation cooperates with the U.S. on counterterrorism efforts because he will have become very familiar with things like how willing the host nation is to provide name checks against vehicle license plates involved in suspicious incidents. Based on these kinds of principles, the indicators are grouped under the following 5 types of Indicator Specialists: Terrorists' Targets Indicator Specialist (TTIS), Chemical Indicator Specialist (CIS), Biological Indicator Specialist (BIS), Nuclear & Radiological Indicator Specialist (NRIS), and Terrorist-Network Indicator Specialist (TIS) (as shown in table 1.6. Staffing Plan: Analyst Positions by Indicators). If an analyst is responsible for assessing many indicators, then he only does so for a small group of countries (and corresponding terrorist groups). If an analyst is responsible for assessing only 1 indicator, then he does so for a large group of countries (and corresponding terrorist groups). Thus, the assignment of these analysts' responsibilities is based primarily on logical groupings of indicators rather than groups of countries.

Table 1.6. Staffing Plan: Analyst Positions by Indicators

TERRORIST CAPABILITY INDICATORS		
Strategic (Countrywide) Indicators	Priority	Indicator Specialist/Analyst
Lethal Agent/Technique		
1. Biological	1	Biological Indicator Specialist
2. Nuclear	1	Nuclear & Radiological Indicator Specialist
3. Radiological	2	
4. Chemical	2	Chemical Indicator Specialist
5. Conventional Bombing/Explosion	2	Terrorist-Network Indicator Specialist
6. Hijacking	2	
7. Hostage Taking/Kidnapping	2	
8. Assassination	3	
9. Firearms	3	
10. Knives/Blades	3	
11. Computer Network Attack (CNA)	3	
12. Miscellaneous*	NA	
Delivery Method	Priority	
13. Ground-Based Vehicle	NA	
14. Water Vessel/Scuba	NA	
15. Aircraft	NA	
16. Missile, Surface-to-Surface	NA	
17. Missile, Surface-to-Air	NA	
18. Missile, Air-to-Surface	NA	
19. Missile, Air-to-Air	NA	
20. Missile, Unknown Type	NA	
21. Suicide Terrorist/Human Host	NA	
22. Mail/Post	NA	
23. Food/Beverages/Water Supply	NA	
24. Gaseous	NA	
25. Miscellaneous*	NA	
TERRORIST INTENTION INDICATORS		
Strategic (Countrywide) Indicators	Priority	
26. Weapons/Material Movement	1	
27. Terrorist Travel	1	
28. Intentionally Left Blank	1	
29. Intentionally Left Blank	1	
30. Terrorist Training	1	
31. Anti-Indicators	1 or Trump	
32. Intentionally Left Blank	2	
33. Intentionally Left Blank	2	
34. Intentionally Left Blank	2	
35. Intentionally Left Blank	2	
36. Intentionally Left Blank	2	
37. Intentionally Left Blank	3	
38. Intentionally Left Blank	3	
39. Intentionally Left Blank	3	
40. Significant Events & Dates in Next 30 Days	3	
41. Intentionally Left Blank	3	
42. Propaganda Levels	3	
43. Miscellaneous*	NA	

Continued on next page

Table 1.6. Staffing Plan: Analyst Positions by Indicators Continued

Tactical (Target Specific) Indicators	Priority	Indicator Specialist/Analyst
44. Surveillance, Physical	1	Terrorists' Targets
45. Intentionally Left Blank	1	Indicator Specialist
46. Intentionally Left Blank	1	
47. Intentionally Left Blank	1	
48. Anti-Indicators	1 or Trump	
49. Test of Security	2	
50. Intentionally Left Blank	2	
51. Intentionally Left Blank	2	
52. Intentionally Left Blank	2	
53. Intentionally Left Blank	3	
54. Intentionally Left Blank	3	
55. Intentionally Left Blank	3	
56. Intentionally Left Blank	3	
57. Intentionally Left Blank	3	
58. Miscellaneous*	NA	
TARGET VULNERABILITY INDICATORS		
Tactical (Target Specific) Indicators	**Priority**	
59. Current Security Posture/FPCON	1	
60. Number of People in Target Area (Damage Level Capacity)	1	
61. Facility Vulnerability Assessment (VA)	2	
62. Significance of Target	3	
63. Miscellaneous*	NA	
Strategic (Countrywide) Indicators	**Priority**	
64. Country's Ability to Deter and Disrupt Terrorist Activity	1	
65. Country's Intent To Deter and Disrupt Terrorist Activity	1	
66. Country's Cooperation with the U.S.	2	
67. Significant Events & Dates in Next 30 Days	2	
68. Miscellaneous*	NA	

Table 1.7 (Staffing Plan: Analyst Positions by Region) shows how many of each type of Indicator Specialist are required for worldwide coverage. Since the Chemical Indicator Specialist (CIS), Biological Indicator Specialist (BIS), and Nuclear & Radiological Indicator Specialist (NRIS) are each responsible for just 1 indicator, they are assigned worldwide coverage. Since the Terrorists' Targets Indicator Specialist (TTIS) is responsible for many indicators, this type of Indicator Specialist is only assigned a limited group of countries within a given region or regions of the world (North America, Latin America-Caribbean, Europe, Africa, East Asia-Pacific, or South Asia-Middle East). For the same reason, the Terrorist-Network Indicator Specialist (TIS) positions are also divided out by those regions of the world. Additionally, the number of Terrorist-Network Indicator Specialist (TIS) positions varies for each region of the world depending on the number of terrorist networks active in a given region. These numbers are a starting point and can be adjusted as necessary. The number of Terrorist-Network Indicator Specialist (TIS) positions is based not only on the requirement to varies for each region of the world depending on the number of terrorist networks active in a given region. These analyst numbers are a starting point and can be adjusted as necessary.

Table 1.7. Staffing Plan: Analyst Positions by Region

	Number of Analysts	North America	Latin America-Caribbean	Europe	Africa	East Asia-Pacific	South Asia-Middle East
Total Number of Analysts	**107**						
Raw Reporting Profiler (RRP)	84	84 Raw Reporting Profilers (RRPs) to profile about 2500 raw intelligence reports daily.					
Senior Warning Officer (SWO)	5	SWO-1	SWO-1	SWO-1	SWO-1	SWO-1	
Terrorists' Targets Indicator Specialist (TTIS)	5	TTIS-1	TTIS-1	TTIS-1	TTIS-1	TTIS-1	
Chemical Indicator Specialist (CIS)	1	CIS-1					
Biological Indicator Specialist (BIS)	1	BIS-1					
Nuclear & Radiological Indicator Specialist (NRIS)	1	NRIS-1					
Terrorist-Network Indicator Specialist (TIS)							
Muslim Terrorist Networks	6	TIS-1	TIS-1	TIS-1	TIS-1	TIS-1	TIS-1
Non-Muslim Terrorist Networks	4	TIS-1	TIS-1	TIS-1	TIS-1		

Senior Warning Officers

Job Description

Senior Warning Officers are a small group of senior analysts who are responsible for ensuring the warning levels are consistent with the available evidence/raw intelligence reports. Senior Warning Officers' duties are:

1. Monitoring and approving all the warning levels that the computer application automatically produces and updates on the webpages. Whenever a Senior Warning Officer rejects a warning level that the system produces, he is required to write a justification in the appropriate *Indicator, Target,* or *Country Warning Narrative: What We Know, Think, & Need to Know,* (as explained in tasks 19, 20, and 21 of the methodology).

2. Writing and maintaining executive summaries for the *Target* and *Country Warning Narrative: What We Know, Think, & Need to Know* webpages for the targets and countries within their area of responsibility (as explained in tasks 20 and 21 of the methodology).

3. Generating additional Collection Requests that become apparent when all the intelligence related to a target or country are drawn together in a *Target* or *Country Warning Narrative: What We Know, Think, & Need to Know* webpage report (as explained in tasks 20 and 21 of the methodology).

4. Writing the analytical comments for the target and country trend analysis webpage pictures that the partly automated methodology produces monthly (as explained in tasks 16, 17, and 18 of the methodology).

5. Briefing decision makers on the warning levels as necessary (as explained in tasks 22 and 23 of the methodology).

6. Determining annually with Indicator Specialists if any new indicators need to be estab-

lished (as explained in task 1 of the methodology) by:

1) Reviewing the raw intelligence reports filed under the Miscellaneous Indicators to determine if any kinds of significant terrorist activity have been overlooked.
2) Reviewing U.S. collection capabilities to determine if the U.S. has gained the capability to collect on any additional terrorist activities.
3) Reviewing case studies of terrorist operations to identify changes in terrorist modus operandi and determine if terrorists are conducting any new activities that the U.S. can collect against.

Although this may seem like an unusually high amount of low-level work for a senior level analyst, it is necessary in order to truly develop his understanding of the big picture.

Explanation of Number Required

Five Senior Warning Officers are required. Since Senior Warning Officers function to fuse the Indicator Specialists' analysis for various targets and countries, and the goal is to enable Senior Warning Officers to do comparison analysis, they are assigned multiple countries within a given region or regions as shown in table 1.7 (Staffing Plan: Analyst Positions by Region). Again, the number of Senior Warning Officers is a starting point estimate and can be adjusted if necessary.

Total Number of Terrorism I&W Analysts Is Far Less Than Current Number

The total staff of 107 analysts (85 Raw Reporting Profilers, 18 Indicator Specialists, and 5 Senior Warning Officers) may seem like a steep requirement, but again, that is far less than the Intelligence Community currently has working to provide worldwide terrorism Indications & Warning assessments. Furthermore, the 107 analysts would guard against 82 percent of 42 common warning pitfalls by operating this methodology, which leads to the evaluation of this methodology against the 42 common warning pitfalls.

Notes

1. The author completed most of the daily tasks in an earlier version of the website, without automated assistance, for 6 countries in Southwest Asia while deployed to Saudi Arabia between August 2000 and July 2001. The process took about 4 hours each morning.
2. James J. McDevitt, "Summary of Indicator-Based-Methodology," unpublished handout, n.p., n.d. provided in January 2002 at the Joint Military Intelligence College. Cited hereafter as McDevitt, "Summary of Indicator-Based-Methodology."
3 The indicators were derived from a synthesis of Sources: "Al Qaeda Manual," *United States Department of Justice*, www.usdoj.gov/ag/trainingmanual.htm (21 Apr. 2002); Charles E. Allen, "Warning and Iraq's Invasion of Kuwait: A Retrospective Look," *Defense Intelligence Journal* 7, no. 2 (Fall 1998): 41; "CNN Presents: Investigating Terror," on CNN, produced by CNN, October 2001; "CNN Saturday Morning News, Interview With John Carroll," *CNN*, www.cnn.com, aired 20 October 2001, under the "Transcripts" link (6 Jun. 2002); Crystal Square Apartments Management, subject: "Building Security Advisory for Real Estate Owners and Managers of Residential Property: FBI General Threat Information for Residential Property Owners/Managers," 20 May 2002; Federal Bureau of Investigation (FBI), *Terrorism in the United States 1998* (Washington D.C.: FBI, 1998), 6; Steve Hooper, Special Agent, Counterterrorism Division, FBI, interview by the author, 12 February 2002; Interagency OPSEC Support Staff, "Operations Security (OPSEC),"

Employees' Guide to Security Responsibilities, rf-web.tamu.edu/files/SECGUIDE/S2unclas/Opsec.htm (5 Jun. 2002); William Matthews, "In the System: Do commercial firms have the data needed to fight terrorism?" *Federal Computer Week*, 11 January 2002, 24; Judith Miller and Don Van Natta Jr., "White House Asked F.B.I. About Unreported Threats," *New York Times*, 23 May, 2002; Niel A. Lewis, "F.B.I. Chief Admits 9/11 Might Have Been Detectable," *New York Times*, 30 May 2002, *The New York Times on the Web* (31 May 2002); Michael Potts, Special Agent, Counterterrorism Division, FBI, interview by the author, 12 February 2002; Survey, "Prioritization of Terrorism Indicator Categories," conducted by the author, January 2002; Leon Drouin Keith, "Calif. Bridge Subject of Alert," *South Coast Today*, 1 November 2002, www.s-t.com/daily/11-01/11-02-01/a01wn006.htm (19 Jul. 2002); United States Department of State, *Patterns of Global Terrorism 2000* (Washington, D.C.: Office of the Secretary of State, 2001), 36.

4. CAPT Tom Facer, USN, Instructor at the Joint Military Intelligence Training Center, Defense Intelligence Agency, interview by the author, 2 September 2002.

5. The author is aware that there are more indicators of target vulnerability than listed in table 1.4, but has not listed them because they are accounted for in the Facility Vulnerability Assessment (VA) Indicator. Counterintelligence agencies write Facility Vulnerability Assessments (VAs), which assess facilities according to those indicators.

6. Doug Whetstone, "Building an Attack Template," briefing presented at the FBI, Washington, D.C., November 2002.

7. "Members of the Intelligence Community (IC)," *United States Intelligence Community – Who We Are* 9 November 2003, www.intelligence.gov/1-members.shtml (2 February 2004).

8. 2500 is the author's high estimate. The author believes 2000 is a more likely estimate, but wants to estimate high to be safe for resource planning purposes, such as the Staffing Plan for this methodology.

9. Tandra Turner and Erin Whitworth showed the author how to create input forms with the Microsoft Access Database program during multiple discussions in November 2002. Gurumeet Kaur Khalsa assisted the author again in August 2004.

10. Employee at Counter Intelligence Field Activity (CIFA), Arlington, Virginia, interview by the author, November 2003.

11. McCarthy, 21.

12. An axiom professed in the "Counterdrug Analysis Course," (Washington, D.C.: Joint Military Intelligence College, August 2002).

13 "Counterdrug Intelligence Analysis," lecture presented in CDIAC class at the Joint Military Intelligence Training Center, Washington, D.C., August 2002.

14. Morgan D. Jones, *The Thinker's Tool Kit: Fourteen Skills for Making Smarter Decisions in Business and in Life* (New York: Random House, 1995), 164.

15. Kam, 122.

16. References in this text to color coding refer to the accompanying CD webpages and not to the screen captures of those webpages reproduced in this book.

17. *Colin Powell on I&W: Address to the Department of Defense Warning Working Group*, distributed by the Joint Military Intelligence College, Washington, D.C., 1991, videocassette. Cited hereafter as Powell.

18. McDevitt, "Summary of Indicator-Based-Methodology."

19. Russo, 135.

20. This principle is evident from the "Warning Paradox." The warning paradox occurs when analysts accurately predict a threat, and a decision maker's consequent security response causes the aggressor to cancel, delay, or redirect the attack, which in turn makes the analysts' prediction appear incorrect. That in turn degrades the decision maker's confidence in the analysts' future assessments. Jan Goldman, *Intelligence Warning Terminology*, (Washington, D.C.: Joint Military Intelligence College, 2001), 40. Cited hereafter as *Intelligence Warning Terminology*.

21. *Colin Powell on I&W: Address to the Department of Defense Warning Working Group*, distributed by the Joint Military Intelligence College, Washington, D.C., 1991, videocassette. Cited hereafter as Powell.

22. Russo, 14.

23. Russo, 135.

24. Author's observations while stationed in Riyadh, Saudi Arabia for the year August 2000 to August 2001.

25. The author conducted this case study and trend analysis while stationed in Riyadh.

26. McDevitt, "Summary of Indicator-Based-Methodology."

27. "CNN Presents: Investigating Terror," on CNN, produced by CNN, October 2001. William Matthews, "In the System: Do commercial firms have the data needed to fight terrorism?" *Federal Computer*

Week, 11 January 2002, 24.

28. McCarthy, 24.

29. Dr. Ben Shneiderman, Professor of Computer Science at the University of Maryland, Abstract to the National Security Agency, subject: "The Eyes Have It: User Interfaces for Information Visualization," 3 April 2002, attachment to e-mail from David T. Moore, NSA, Analyst, MD to author, 3 April 2002. Cited hereafter as Shneiderman, "The Eyes Have It."

30. Charles E. Allen, "Warning and Iraq's Invasion of Kuwait: A Retrospective Look," *Defense Intelligence Journal* 7, no. 2 (Fall 1998): 43. Cited hereafter as Allen.

31. Seth Godin, "Applying Old Marketing Rules to the Cyber World," *Business Week Book Excerpt*, *Business Week Online* 1999, www.businessweek.com/smallbiz/news/coladvice/book/bk990709.htm (30 May 2002). Cited hereafter as Godin, "Applying Old Marketing Rules to the Cyber World."

32. CDR Steven Carey, USN, "Strategic Warning and Threat Management," lecture presented in ANA680 class at the Joint Military Intelligence College (JMIC), Washington, D.C., February 2002. Cited hereafter as JMIC "Strategic Warning" course.

33. Allen, 35.

34. Powell.

35. National Warning Staff, DCI Warning Committee, "National Warning System," handout provided in January 2002 at the Joint Military Intelligence College.

36. Joint Information Systems Committee (JISC), "Project Management/Introduction: 1.2 Why do Projects Fail?" *JISC infoNet* 2004, http://www.jiscinfonet.ac.uk/InfoKits/project-management/pm-intro-1.2 (23 Feb. 2004).

37. Kenneth C. Laudon and Jane P. Laudon, *Management Information Systems: Organization and Technology in Network Enterprise, 4th ed* (Upper Saddle River, NJ: Prentice-Hall, 2001), 288.

38. 2500 is the author's high estimate. The author believes 2000 is a more likely estimate, but wants to estimate high to be safe for resource planning purposes, such as the Staffing Plan for this methodology.

39. Employee at Counter Intelligence Field Activity (CIFA), Arlington, Virginia, interview by the author, November 2003.

Chapter 2

The Acid Test:
Evaluation of the Methodology against
the 42 Common Warning Pitfalls

The test of a first-rate intelligence is the ability to hold two opposite ideas in mind at the same time and still retain the ability to function.
F. Scott Fitzgerald

This warning methodology guards against 33 of the 42 common warning pitfalls, provides a partial guard against 3 pitfalls, and provides no guard against 6 pitfalls, which averages to an 82 percent guard against the pitfalls. The primary purpose of considering a new warning methodology is to determine if it will improve warning. A reasonable approach is to evaluate the methodology's ability to guard against common pitfalls that have hindered warning in the past.

Warning experts have identified and recorded 42 common warning pitfalls in their case studies of warning failures in history.[1] These case studies include, but are not limited to: the 1940 German Blitzkrieg against France; the 1941 German attack on Russia; the 1941 Japanese attack on Pearl Harbor; the 1942 Japanese attack on the British in Malaya, Singapore; the 1942 failed British-Canadian attack on the Germans at Dieppe; the 1944 D-Day Landings; the 1950 North Korean invasion of South Korea; the 1950 Chinese Intervention in Korea; the 1956 Israeli attack on Egypt's Sinai Peninsula; the 1962 Chinese attack on India; the 1967 Israeli attack on Egypt; the 1968 Tet Offensive in Vietnam; the 1973 Yom Kippur War; the 1978 fall of the Shah of Iran; the 1982 Falklands War; the 1991 Iraqi attack on Kuwait; the 1994 Humanitarian Crisis in Rwanda.[2]

The pitfalls are grouped in this study according to which phase of Indications & Warning they plague. Two pitfalls affect Phase I (Identify Key Elements of the Intelligence Problem); 2 pitfalls impede Phase II (Consolidate Information); 9 pitfalls hinder Phase III (Sort Information); 15 pitfalls obstruct Phase IV (Draw Conclusions); 2 pitfalls restrain Phase V (Focus Collectors on Intelligence Gaps to Refine/Update Conclusions); and 12 pitfalls inhibit Phase VI (Communicate Conclusions/Give Warning). Table 2.1 lists the common warning pitfalls and indicates which of the 23 tasks in the methodology guard against which pitfalls.

Table 2.1. Overview Evaluation of Methodology against the 42 Common Warning Pitfalls

#	I&W Phases & Associated Pitfalls	Assessment	Tasks that guard
	**Guard against 33, Partial Guard against 3, No Guard against 6**		
	PHASE I: Define/Validate Key Elements of Problem	*With Indicators*	
1	Selecting Indicators Is Subject to Intuitive Shortcomings	Partial	1, 10
2	The Pitfall of the Indicator Paradox	Guard	6, 10-15
	PHASE II: Consolidate Information	*With Master Database*	
3	Unintentional Fractionalized Distribution of Information	Guard	5, 6
4	Intentional Fractionalized Distribution of Information	No Guard	
	PHASE III: Sort Information	*With Hypothesis Matrices*	
5	Indicators Filter Out Pertinent Information	Guard	6, 10-15, 1
6	Interpreting Ambiguous Information as Endorsing Favorite Hypothesis	Guard	6-15
7	Bias	Guard	6-15
8	Bolstering	Guard	6-15
9	Undermining	Guard	6-15
10	Differentiation	Guard	6-15
11	Ignoring	Guard	6-15
12	The Mind Is Overwhelmed with Information	Guard	6-15
13	Information Appears Insignificant on Its Own	Guard	6-9
	PHASE IV: Draw Conclusions	*With Intuitive & Structured Techniques*	
14	Generating and Assessing Hypotheses Via Deduction	Guard	6, 7
15	Generating and Assessing Hypotheses Via Induction	Guard	10-15
16	"Scenarios (Hypotheses) Create Mindsets"	Guard	6, 7
17	Tendency to Stick to First Conclusion	Guard	6-15
18	Linear Model Hypothesis Testing Is Inconsistent with the Highly Accepted Chaos Theory	Guard	1, 6, 7, 10-15
19	The Availability Heuristic	Guard	7, 16-18
20	The Representativeness Heuristic	Partial	16-18
21	The Anchoring and Adjustment Heuristic	Guard	8-15
22	Deception: A-Type	Guard	6, 7
23	Deception: M-Type	No Guard	
24	Deception: Active	No Guard	
25	Deception: Passive (Also Known As "Creeping Normalcy" or "Desensitization")	Guard	6, 7, 10
26	Assessment Does Not Account for Defender's Ability to Protect Against Attacker's Capability	Guard	13, 14, 1
27	Assessment Does Not Account for a Target's Changing Circumstances	Guard	10, 13, 14
28	Failing to Account for Gaps in Intelligence Collection Coverage	Guard	10
	PHASE V: Focus Collectors On Intelligence Gaps to Refine/Update Conclusions	*With Collection Requests in Narrative Assessments*	
29	Failing to Focus Intelligence Collection on Gaps in Intelligence	Guard	3, 10, 19-21
30	Focusing Intelligence Collection on Information that Supports Favorite Hypothesis	Guard	3, 8, 10, 19-21
	PHASE VI: Communicate Conclusions/Warning	*With Website Display*	
31	Communication Not Convincing	Guard	7, 8, 10-18, 22
32	Communication Not Clear	Guard	10-15
33	Communication Not Concise	Guard	7, 10-15
34	Communication Not Timely	Guard	10-15
35	The Pitfall of the Warning Dilemma	Guard	10
36	The Pitfall of the Warning Paradox	Partial	16-18
37	"The Super Analyst"	Guard	7, 10-15
38	Decision Maker Has Access to Other Information	Partial	5, 6, 7
39	Assessment Does Not Support Decision Maker's Policy	No Guard	
40	Fear of Provocation	No Guard	
41	Decision Maker Bias	No Guard	
42	Intelligence Products Not Focused on Warning	Guard	6, 7, 10-18, 23

Assessment of
Phase I (Define/Validate Key Elements of Problem):
Guard against 1 of 2 Common Pitfalls; Partial Guard against 1

1. Selecting Indicators Is Subject to Intuitive Shortcomings

Description of Pitfall

Analysts must use intuition when selecting indicators, "those [collectable] things that would have to happen and those that would likely happen as [a] scenario unfolded."[3] However, research shows that intuitive judgments "seldom take proper account of all the information available."[4] People selectively remember information based on the vividness and recency of their exposure to it. "People have difficulty keeping more than seven or so 'chunks' of information in mind at once."[5] Psychological studies show that people tend to ignore evidence that does not support their biases and interpret ambiguous information as confirming their biases. When the mind is overwhelmed with information, that tendency is magnified as part of a simplification technique to reduce the information down to a manageable size.[6] Furthermore, "intuitive judgments suffer from serious random inconsistencies due to fatigue, boredom, and all the factors that make us human."[7] Therefore, intuition can cause analysts to create a list of indicators that is not representative of all the evidence.[8]

Partial Guard against Pitfall

Tasks 1 and 10 of the methodology partially guard against this pitfall by using a systematic process to guide analysts' intuitive selection of indicators. "Considerable research suggests that you will maximize your chances of making the best [intuitive] choice if you find a systematic way to evaluate all the evidence."[9] On an *annual basis*, in task 1, analysts determine if they should alter the list of Terrorism Indicators shown in table 1.4 by: 1) reviewing the raw intelligence reports in the Miscellaneous Indicators to determine if any kinds of significant terrorist activity have been overlooked, 2) reviewing U.S. collection capabilities to determine if the U.S. has gained or lost the capability to collect on any terrorist activities, and 3) reviewing case studies of terrorist operations to identify changes in terrorist modus operandi and determine if terrorists are conducting any new activities that the U.S. can collect against. As analysts create the list of indicators according to that process, they record their rationale and supporting sources for each indicator on the Indicators-Rationale Log webpage shown in (figure 1.2). This log helps analysts divide information and key judgments into logical simplified parts with less information to digest at once. Furthermore, the fact that the rationale is available on a webpage for all other analysts to review provides for a system of checks and balances.

Additionally, on a *daily basis*, in task 10, analysts review the new information in the Miscellaneous Indicators to determine if any new indicators should be established. Analysts use the questions in the Miscellaneous Indicator Key Questions, Answers, & Evidence Log (shown in figure 1.10) to assist them in making that determination. If an analyst believes there is information in a Miscellaneous Indicator that warrants creating a new indicator, he submits a proposal to other terrorism experts to create a new indicator. Both tasks 1 and 10 provide consistent checks and balances on the latest list of indicators, which continuously upgrades the list of indicators to better represent all the evidence. This, however, is only a partial guard because even a systematic process does not eliminate all the weaknesses of intuition.

2. The Pitfall of the Indicator Paradox

Description of Pitfall

The Indicator Paradox can cause either deficient or overly complex assessments. The Indicator Paradox is that: if analysts select too many indicators, their methodology will be too complex to track and comprehend; but if analysts select too few indicators, their methodology will be deficient/inaccurate. Thus, the warning pitfall of the Indicator Paradox is that: 1) analysts develop deficient/inaccurate warning assessments because they selected too few indicators in an effort to keep their methodology easy to track and comprehend, or 2) analysts develop overly complex warning assessments because they have selected too many indicators in effort to make their methodology accurate.[10]

Guard against Pitfall

Tasks 6 and 10-15 guard against this pitfall because they display information/assessments on webpages, which are renowned for enabling people to display large sets of data clearly—thus allowing analysts to select as many indicators as necessary. Graphic interface experts have found that the most effective way to capitalize on human perceptual skills is to show "overview first, [then] zoom and filter, and then details-on-demand."[11] The warning assessments/pictures in the website follow that design principle via 3 primary types of warning picture views: 1) country list view, 2) target list view, and 3) indicator list view (of terrorist intentions, terrorist capability, or target vulnerability), as shown in figure 1.1 (The 3 Primary Warning Picture Views). From an indicator list view, people can select various categories of indicator information that are plainly identified under table headings—such as "Relevant Raw Reports," and "Indicator Key Questions, Answers, & Evidence Logs" (as shown in figure 1.6). Narrative assessments follow the same overall hierarchy under headings marked for countries, targets, and indicators (as shown in figure 1.19). Furthermore, the display of indicators is also simplified by dividing them into the 3 sub-groupings of risk—adversary intentions, adversary capability, and target vulnerability. Therefore, analysts can select as many indicators as necessary to make the methodology and assessments as accurate as possible, while still keeping the assessments easy to follow and comprehend.

Assessment of
Phase II (Consolidate Information):
Guard against 1 of 2 Common Pitfalls

3. Unintentional Fractionalized Distribution of Information

Description of Pitfall

No single person or analysis unit is able to see the entire intelligence puzzle because dissemination from numerous collection agencies is disjointed.[12] Fractionalized distribution of information was a key factor in 2 of the United States's most devastating homeland surprise attacks: Pearl Harbor and the September 11, 2001 terrorist attacks.

Guard against Pitfall

Task 5 and 6 guard against this pitfall. In task 5, all fifteen Member Organizations of the Intelligence Community and other federal U.S. organizations that may have terrorism-related information are required to forward *all* their terrorism-related raw intelligence reports to an *Intelligence Community Master Database*. Additionally, the FBI would consolidate suspicious incident reports from local law enforcement agencies, private security companies, commercial firms, and private citizens to forward to the queue. Then in task 6, analysts are required to enter *all* those reports into a Terrorism Forecasting Database. Thus all the U.S. Intelligence Community's raw terrorism intelligence reports are consolidated and organized in an easily searched forum.

4. Intentional Fractionalized Distribution of Information

Description of Pitfall

No single person or analysis unit is able to see all the pieces of the intelligence puzzle because security is too tight or because a collection agency refuses to cooperate. In the Pearl Harbor case, "security was so tight [on Magic intercepts], that no one was allowed to keep a complete file of the messages."[13] Thus readers were forced to "[scan] the messages rapidly while the officer in charge of delivery stood by to take the copy back again."[14] Consequently, "no one ever reviewed the entire series of messages . . . and no single intercept was striking enough to change the established views." [15] In another situation, "when Lieutenant Commander Edwind Layton, who was in charge of fleet intelligence, requested access to diplomatic intelligence for his own estimates, he was refused, first on the grounds of security, and second on the grounds of duplication."[16]

No Guard against Pitfall

The methodology does not guard against this pitfall. If regulations prohibit information sharing, then the master database will be incomplete and fractionalized distribution of information will persist. Alternatively, if regulations call for information sharing, but an organization does not comply, then the master database will be incomplete and fractionalized distribution of information will still persist.

Assessment of
Phase III (Sort Information):
Guard against 9 of 9 Common Pitfalls

5. Indicators Filter Out Pertinent Information

Description of Pitfall

Analysts filter out/discard pertinent information that does not fit into the list of predetermined indicators.[17] An indicator list is a proven tool to help analysts distinguish signals (pertinent information) from noise (impertinent information). However, if an indicator list is incomplete, it can cause analysts to accidentally filter out pertinent information. An indicator list could be incomplete due to changes in enemy modus operandi, changes in intelligence collection capabilities, or analysts neglecting evidence when they created the indicator list.

Guard against Pitfall

Tasks 6, 10-15, and 1 guard against this pitfall. In task 6, analysts use "Miscellaneous Indicators" to file indications that do not fit into any of the existing indicators. In task 10, analysts re-

view the information in the Miscellaneous Indicators on a daily basis to determine if any new indicators should be established. Analysts use the questions in the Miscellaneous Indicator Key
Questions, Answers, & Evidence Log (shown in figure 1.10) to assist them in making that determination. If an analyst believes there is information in a Miscellaneous Indicator that warrants
creating a new indicator, he submits a proposal to create a new indicator. If other terrorism experts
approve the new indicator, then the analyst assesses its Indicator Activity Level in task 10. Then,
in tasks 11-15, the computer application uses the new indicator's Indicator Activity Level along
with all the other indicators' Indicator Activity Levels to determine the Target Risk Warning Levels and Country Risk Warning Levels. Thus the pertinent information is not discarded from assessments. Task 1 further guards against this pitfall because analysts meet annually to review the
reports in the Miscellaneous Indicators to determine if any new indicators need to be established.
A new indicator could be warranted due to changes in U.S. collection capabilities or changes in
the adversary's modus operandi.

6. Interpreting Ambiguous Information as Endorsing Favorite Hypothesis

Description of Pitfall

Analysts view ambiguous information as endorsing their favorite hypothesis and do not apply
the information the other hypotheses with which it is also consistent.[18] In other words, analysts
"tend to overlook the fact that evidence they regard as supporting their hypothesis may also be
consistent with several alternative hypotheses."[19]

Guard against Pitfall

Tasks 6 and 7 guard against this pitfall. In task 6, analysts file all incoming raw intelligence
reports, including ambiguous information, under every indicator, target, country, and terrorist
network to which it applies. Then in task 7, the computer program displays the information in
every hypothesis matrix to which it applies, so the information does not support 1 applicable hypothesis over the other.

7. Bias

Description of Pitfall

Bias is "an inclination . . . that inhibits impartial judgment [of facts and information]."[20] Intelligence warning experts have identified numerous biases that cause analysts to misjudge information. These biases include but are not limited to: mirror imaging, overconfidence, group think,
vividness, favor of causal explanation (popularity of conspiracy theories), and favoring perception
of centralized direction.[21] Although the biases have different rationales, they have the same end
result: misjudging facts and information.

Guard against Pitfall

Since biases all yield the same end result, misjudging information, a protection against the effects of misjudging information can guard against the various biases. *Tasks 6-15 protect against
the effects of analysts' misjudging information.* There are 2 effects of misjudging facts and information: discarding the information and discounting/miscalculating the significance of the information.

Alternatively, if analysts want to *discard* a raw intelligence report, they cannot because in task

6 of the methodology, analysts are required to enter every terrorism-related raw intelligence report from the Intelligence Community Master Database into the Terrorism Forecasting Database. In tasks 7 and 8, the computer application automatically displays all the reports under all the hypothesis matrices (and corresponding indicators and key questions) to which the reports apply. Analysts cannot remove reports from the database or the hypothesis matrices. Instead, in task 9, the computer application italicizes the hyperlinks to reports that meet at least one of six strict rules for being *discounted* from an assessment: 1) the threat expires, 2) officials eliminate the threat, 3) officials determine through investigation that the threat/incident was benign, 4) the source is judged about 10 percent credible, or 5) the information is judged about 10 percent feasible/viable.

Secondly, if analysts try to *discount/miscalculate the significance* of a *pertinent* report on a hypothesis, the methodology hinders them in 3 ways. First, in task 9, when analysts decide to discount a report from an assessment, they are required to provide a justification for the "Analyst Comment" section of the report's webpage display. In doing so, the analyst must check a box in the database to indicate 1 of the 5 acceptable reasons for discounting a report, or the database will not accept the analyst's input (and will not italicize the report hyperlink on the hypothesis matrix webpage display). The analysts must also write additional commentary on 1 of these 5 acceptable reasons for discounting a report: 1) the threat expires (such as a report stating terrorists intended to attack before the end of the New Year, but the date passes for several months without incident); 2) officials eliminate the threat (such as FBI officials apprehending a suspected terrorist who had reportedly traveled into the country), 3) officials determine through investigation that the threat/incident was benign (such as officials discovering that the person who photographed a nuclear facility was actually part of a government contracted risk assessment team), 4) the *collector* has determined that the source is not credible (because in *most* [not all] cases, the collector naturally knows the source [and his reporting history] better than the analyst); or 5) the information is not feasible/viable/"*does not make logical sense*," which is different from the unacceptable reason that the analyst thinks the information is *unlikely*.[22] The requirement for an analyst to provide the justification for dismissing a report according to 1 of the 5 prescribed reasons helps the analyst ensure his reasoning is based on logic rather than this pitfall. For instance, if the analyst is mirror imaging, that will likely become apparent in his written justification for discarding the report. Furthermore, the fact that the justification is available on the report webpage for all other analysts to review provides for a system of checks and balances.

Second, in task 8 the computer displays each raw report as evidence next to each relevant hypothesis question in the Indicator Key Questions, Answers, & Evidence Log webpages. That format of displaying the information would highlight an analyst's misjudgment in an answer to a question as a blatant error. Again, the fact that the information is available on the report webpage for all other analysts to review provides for a system of checks and balances.

Third, in task 10, the computer averages the answers to all the questions in the Indicator Key Questions, Answers, & Evidence Log to determine the Indicator Activity Level, which the computer later uses to calculate the Target Risk Warning Level and Country Risk Warning Level in tasks 11-15. Those automatic computer calculations deny analysts the opportunity to discount the value of information on a hypothesis. If analysts decide to overwrite a computer calculation, they are required to write a justification to be displayed on the website, which adds another layer to the guard against this pitfall.

8. Bolstering

Description of Pitfall

Analysts discard pertinent information or discount the significance of pertinent information that is inconsistent with their favorite hypothesis by rationalizing "let's wait for awhile" to include this information, while the analysts pursue or wait for other information that will support their favorite hypothesis.[23] Thus the analysts hope to later bolster their favorite hypothesis with other information in order to negate the importance of the discrepant information. This ultimately causes analysts to develop a warning assessment that is not representative of all the evidence.[24]

Guard against Pitfall

As explained in pitfall 7, tasks 6-15 protect against discarding or discounting the significance of information on an assessment.

9. Undermining

Description of Pitfall

Analysts discard pertinent information or discount the significance of pertinent information that is inconsistent with their favorite hypothesis by rationalizing that either 1) the *source* of information is not credible or 2) there is some other underlying flaw in the information (such as deception).[25] Thus analysts undermine the information by rejecting some quality of the information. This ultimately causes analysts to develop a warning assessment that is not representative of all the evidence.[26]

Guard against Pitfall

As explained in pitfall 7, tasks 6-15 protect against discarding or discounting the significance of information in an assessment.

10. Differentiation

Description of Pitfall

Analysts discard pertinent information or discount the significance of pertinent information that is inconsistent with their favorite hypothesis by rationalizing that the most important part of the information does not necessarily contradict their beliefs and therefore "throw out the rest."[27] This ultimately causes analysts to develop a warning assessment that is not representative of all the evidence.[28]

Guard against Pitfall

As explained in pitfall 7, tasks 6-15 protect against discarding or discounting the significance of information in an assessment.

11. Ignoring

Description of Pitfall

Analysts discard pertinent information or discount the significance of pertinent information that is inconsistent with their favorite hypothesis by rationalizing that this is a "one in a million occurrence . . . maybe it will go away."[29] Thus the analysts "simply live with this puzzle until the outbreak of war."[30] This ultimately causes analysts to develop a warning assessment that is not representative of all the evidence.[31]

Guard against Pitfall

As explained in pitfall 7, tasks 6-15 protect against discarding or discounting the significance of information in an assessment.

12. The Mind Is Overwhelmed with Information

Description of Pitfall

Analysts discard pertinent information or discount the significance of pertinent information because they cannot mentally handle the volume of data. "Numerous studies suggest that people have difficulty keeping more than seven or so 'chunks' of information in mind at once."[32] "Collecting different types of information from various sources and integrating them into an overall judgment is a difficult cognitive process. . . . The problem is complicated since analysts have to examine many pieces of information."[33]

Guard against Pitfall

As explained in pitfall 7, tasks 6-15 protect against discarding or discounting the significance of information in an assessment. Additionally, tasks 6, 7, 8, and 10 guard against this pitfall because they divide information and key judgments into logical simplified parts with less information to digest at once. In tasks 6, 7, and 8 analysts use automated assistance to quickly divide information into indicators and key questions sets within potential target hypothesis matrices. This enables analysts to limit their intuitive judgments to small groups of information within just 1 key question under 1 indicator when they assess an "Indicator Activity Level" in task 10. Then, in tasks 11-15, the *computer application* uses those small "Indicator Activity Level" judgments to build the larger assessments on entire potential target hypotheses, so analysts are not overwhelmed with information.

13. Information Appears Insignificant on Its Own

Description of Pitfall

Analysts discard pertinent information "bit by bit" because it appears insignificant on its own, which prevents analysts from recognizing the significance of the "whole series of signals" in a consolidated context.[34]

Guard against Pitfall

As explained in pitfall 7, tasks 6-9 protect against *discarding* information. Additionally, the hypothesis matrices enable analysts to view every new report in the context of the "whole series of signals." Thus the hypothesis matrices force analysts to look at the entire "ground truth" list of indications altogether. Ultimately, that helps analysts to recognize when signals are mounting to a significant abnormality.

Assessment of
Phase IV (Draw Conclusions):
Guard against 12 of 15 Common Pitfalls;
Partial Guard against 1

14. Generating and Assessing Hypotheses Via Deduction

Description of Pitfall

Analysts use established theories to generate hypotheses, which causes analysts to neglect legitimate hypotheses outside established theories.[35]

Guard against Pitfall

Tasks 6 and 7 guard against this pitfall because they enable incoming reports to generate new hypotheses. In task 6, if a report arrives that does not fall under an existing hypothesis/target or terrorist group listed in the database, then analysts add the new target or terrorist group to the database list. Then in task 7, the database computer application creates a new potential target hypothesis matrix with the new associated report(s)/evidence. Thus, the list of hypotheses is not bound by the analysts' deductive limitations, but rather is free to grow from the actual threat information that is arriving.

15. Generating and Assessing Hypotheses Via Induction

Description of Pitfall

Analysts use a few observations to generate a hypothesis and consequently draw a far-reaching conclusion from the limited amount of evidence.[36]

Guard against Pitfall

Induction is the method used to generate hypotheses (in tasks 6 and 7), but tasks 10-15 guard against drawing far-reaching conclusions without additional evidence. In tasks 10-15 the warning level of a hypothesis matrix cannot increase unless multiple indications/reports in an appropriate number of indicators drive it up. In task 10, after analysts have used the indications/reports to assess answers to the questions in the Indicator Key Questions, Answers, & Evidence Logs, the computer application does not increase an Indicator Activity Level unless the answers to the questions in the logs reach a required threshold. Then in tasks 11-15, the computer application does not increase a hypothesis matrix warning level unless multiple Indicator Warning Levels reach a required threshold. Thus, a limited amount of evidence in a single indicator cannot lead to a far-reaching conclusion, such as a high warning level for a hypothesis matrix.

16. "Scenarios (Hypotheses) Create Mindsets"[37]

Description of Pitfall

Analysts fail to think of new scenarios (fail to generate new hypotheses) because their minds are set on their predetermined list of scenarios/hypotheses. The analysts think their list of hypotheses is a comprehensive representation of all possibilities. The hypotheses act as filters and cause analysts to discard evidence that points to hypotheses they have not imagined.[38]

Guard against Pitfall

Tasks 6 and 7 guard against this pitfall because they enable incoming reports to drive generation of new hypotheses (as explained in pitfall 14). In task 6, if a report arrives that does not fall under an existing hypothesis/target listed in the database, then the analyst adds the new target to the database list. Then in task 7, the database computer application creates a new potential target hypothesis matrix with the new associated report(s)/evidence. Thus, the list of hypotheses is not bound by the analysts' mindsets, but is free to grow from incoming threat information. Evidence is not discarded, but is displayed according to new potential threat scenarios.

17. Tendency to Stick to First Conclusion

Description of Pitfall

Analysts tend to stick to the "the first hypothesis that seems close enough" because "after an image has been formed, new information will not have the same impact it would have had at an earlier stage."[39] It takes more evidence to disprove a favorite hypothesis than to prove it.[40] These effects are magnified when analysts are under crisis and time pressure to reach quick conclusions.[41] This pitfall differs from "Scenarios Create Mindsets" in that the analyst favors just *1* hypothesis (because he believes the evidence supports it); where as in "Scenarios Create Mindsets," the analyst favors a *group* of hypotheses (because he thinks the list is a comprehensive representation of all possibilities).

Guard against Pitfall

Tasks 6-15 guard against this pitfall. New, credible information should have at least 1 of 2 impacts: 1) generate a new hypothesis or 2) weigh appropriately in a hypothesis. Tasks 6 and 7 generate a new hypothesis whenever information arrives that does not fit into an existing hypothesis, as already explained in pitfalls 14 and 16. Tasks 8-15 guard against analysts discounting/miscalculating the significance of a pertinent report on a hypothesis, as already explained in pitfall 7.

Additionally, task 10 guards against this pitfall by limiting an analyst's value judgments on information to *just indicator questions* rather than to an *entire hypothesis*. In task 10, analysts answer questions on an indicator using the raw intelligence reports in the Indicator Key Questions Answers and Evidence Log. That focus on indicator questions makes the analyst partially removed from thinking about whether the report supports or disproves his favorite hypothesis. Rather, he is focused on thinking about whether the report supports or disproves a question on an indicator.

18. Linear Model Hypothesis Testing Is Inconsistent with the Highly Accepted Chaos Theory

Description of Pitfall

Linear model hypothesis testing requires that *all* the indicators of a hypothesis occur and that they occur in a *prescribed order*. However, the highly accepted Chaos Theory rejects both requirements. Furthermore, Chaos Theory requires assessments to acknowledge the potential for *a minor factor to significantly affect a major event,* much like the drop of a single grain of sand can topple a sand pile or the cliché "the straw that broke the camel's back." Chaos Theory requires analysts to *recognize patterns emerging out of chaotic interactions between countless variables*, like grains of sand in an hourglass falling into a symmetric pattern. Chaos Theory requires predictive analysis to *account for unexpected elements (such as new indicators and potential scenarios)* due to interactions between countless random variables.[42]

Guard against Pitfall

Tasks 1, 6, 7, and 10-15 guard against this pitfall. This methodology does not use linear model hypothesis testing. The method of hypothesis testing in this system is consistent with Chaos Theory principles.

Unlike linear model hypothesis testing, this methodology does not require that all indicators of a hypothesis occur or that they occur in a prescribed order. Instead, tasks 10-15 merely require activity in multiple indictors to reach a *threshold* that is set *below* the requirement for activity in *all* the indicators. In task 10, analysts monitor and asses an indictor's activity (based on incoming raw intelligence reports) using an Indicator Key Questions, Answers, & Evidence Log. In this log, analysts answer questions about an indicator's activity on a on a 5-level scale of: 1) "Almost Certainly True (~90%)," about 90 percent probability, color coded red on the website, 2) "Probably True (~70%)," color coded orange, 3) "Probably Not True (~30%)," color coded yellow, 4) "Almost Certainly Not True (~10%)," color coded gray, or 5) "Unknown (or ~50%)," color coded black. Then the computer application averages the answers to those questions to determine an Indicator Activity Level on a 5-level scale of 1) Critical (~90%), about 90 percent probability, color coded red on the website, 2) Significant (~70%), color coded orange, 3) Minor (~30%), color coded yellow, 4) Slight (~10%), color coded gray, and 5) Unknown (or ~50%), color coded black. The computer program then combines the Indicator Activity Level with the indicator's Priority to determine an Indicator Warning Level on a 5-level scale of Critical (~90%), Significant (~70%), Minor (~30%), Slight (~10%), and Unknown (or ~50%). Then in tasks 11-15, the computer program averages the Indicator Warning Levels to determine the hypothesis matrices' warning levels on the 5-level scale of Critical (~90%), Significant (~70%), Minor (~30%), Slight (~10%), and Unknown (or ~50%). The threshold required to increase a hypothesis matrix's warning level to "Critical (~90%)" is set *below* the average of *all* "Critical (~90%)" Indicator Waning Levels. Thus, this method of hypothesis testing does not require that all indicators of a hypothesis occur, or that they occur in a prescribed order, to endorse a hypothesis at the highest warning level.

Tasks 10-15 enable the methodology to allow *a minor factor to significantly affect a major event*. In task 10, *1 piece of evidence* (raw intelligence report) can *increase an entire Target or Country Risk Warning Level* (like the drop of a single grain of sand can topple a sand pile or the cliché "the straw that broke the camel's back"). One piece of evidence can change an answer in an Indicator Key Questions, Answers, & Evidence Log, which can tip the average of the answers in the log up to the threshold of the next higher Indicator Activity Level. That increase in the Indicator Activity Level can lead to a series of threshold breakthroughs in Indicator Warning Level, Terrorist Intention Warning Level, Target Risk Warning Level, and Country Risk Warning Level via tasks 11-15.

Tasks 6 and 7 enable analysts to *recognize patterns emerging out of chaotic interactions between countless variables*. If the thousands of raw intelligence reports that analysts receive daily represent the countless chaotic variables involved in terrorism forecasting, then tasks 6 and 7 put them into a recognizable pattern of terrorist attack preparations (like grains of sand in an hourglass falling into a symmetric pattern). In task 6, analysts enter the raw reports into the Terrorism Forecasting Database; and in doing so, the analysts check lists of boxes to indicate all the terrorist groups, countries, specific targets, indicators, and key questions and that apply to a report. A single raw report may relate to multiple terrorist groups, countries, specific targets, indicators, and key questions. If a report does not fit into any of the existing indicators, the analyst files the report in the appropriate *Other/Miscellaneous* intention, capability, or vulnerability indicator. If a report pertains to a target or terrorist network that is not listed, the analyst can add the target or terrorist network to the list. Then in task 7, the computer program automatically displays the reports under the appropriate Terrorism Indicators and within the appropriate *Potential Target Hypothesis Matrices* [as shown in figure 1.5, Hypothesis Matrix: Indicator List View (with Link to Raw Reports Display)]. Thus the hypothesis matrices created by tasks 6 and 7 enable analysts to recognize patterns of terrorist attack preparations emerging out of the countless chaotic raw intelligence reports that analysts receive daily.

Task 6, 10, and 1 enable analysts to account for *unexpected elements (such as new indicators and potential scenarios)* due to interactions between countless random variables. Tasks 6, 10, and 1 allow for new indicators. On a daily basis, in task 6 analysts file incoming raw intelligence reports that do not fit into the existing indicators, under the appropriate *Other/Miscellaneous* intention, capability, or vulnerability indicator. Then in task 10, analysts review the information in the Miscellaneous Indicators to determine if any new indicators should be established. Analysts use the questions in the Miscellaneous Indicator Key Questions, Answers, & Evidence Log (shown in figure 1.10) to assist them in making that determination. If an analyst believes there is information in a Miscellaneous Indicator that warrants creating a new indicator, he submits a proposal to other terrorism experts to create a new indicator. Additionally, on an annual basis, in task 1, analysts determine if they should add or remove Terrorism Indicators from the list shown in table 1.4 by: 1) reviewing the raw intelligence reports in the Miscellaneous Indicators to determine if any kinds of significant terrorist activity have been overlooked, 2) reviewing U.S. collection capabilities to determine if the U.S. has gained or lost the capability to collect on any terrorist activities, and 3) reviewing case studies of terrorist operations to identify changes in terrorist modus operandi and determine if terrorists are conducting any new activities that the U.S. can collect against. If other terrorism experts approve the new indicator, then the analyst assesses its Indicator Activity Level, and it is factored into the hypothesis warning levels with all the other indicators (as described in tasks 10-15). Thus, analysts account for unexpected elements/indicators due to interactions between countless random variables like changes in modus operandi and changes in U.S. collection capabilities.

Tasks 6 and 7 also allow for unexpected potential scenarios/hypotheses by generating a new hypothesis matrix whenever a piece of evidence arrives that does not fit into the existing hypothesis matrices. In task 6, when analysts enter a report into the Terrorism Forecasting Database, if the report pertains to a target or terrorist group that is not listed, the analyst can add the target or terrorist group to the list. Then in task 7, the computer program automatically creates a new Potential Target Hypothesis Matrix webpage [as shown in figure 1.5, Hypothesis Matrix: Indicator List View (with Link to Raw Reports Display)] and displays a hyperlink to the associated report(s) under the appropriate indicator(s) within the hypothesis matrix. The hypothesis matrix in figure 1.5 shows the indicators and corresponding indications (reports) of a terrorist network's intentions to attack a target in a given country. Thus, tasks 6 and 7 allow for unexpected potential scenarios/hypotheses due to interactions between countless random variables, such as newly selected targets and new terrorist groups.

19. The Availability Heuristic

Description of Pitfall

Heuristics are "inferential rules . . . which reduce difficult mental functions into simpler ones . . . . when faced with the difficult task of assessing the probability and frequency of events and predicting values. . . . Usually heuristics are quite useful and effective; but in some circumstances they lead to systematic and severe errors with serious implications."[43] Psychological experts have identified 3 judgmental heuristics that people employ to assess probabilities and the pitfall associated with each heuristic. The first is called "availability." [44]

The pitfall of the Availability Heuristic is that "people assess the likelihood or frequency of an event by the ease with which relevant instances or occurrences can be brought to mind; . . . . the ease with which things come to mind, however, is affected by many factors unrelated to actual probability."[45]

Guard against Pitfall

Tasks 16-18 guard against this pitfall because they create trend analysis of warning levels for indicators, targets, and countries that show the true frequency of events. This relieves analysts from relying on their memory. Task 7 also guards against this pitfall because it creates the hypothesis matrices that show the true frequency (number) of raw intelligence reports/indications/activity in the indicators [as shown in figure 1.5, Hypothesis Matrix: Indicator List View (with Link to Raw Reports Display)]. Again, this relieves analysts from relying on their memory.

20. The Representativeness Heuristic

Description of Pitfall

Analysts treat a limited sample as representative of an entire body of evidence in order to guide their judgment on the probability of a similar event. Intelligence analysts are particularly subject to this pitfall because "there are only a few relevant events [to reference; so] analysts and policy makers tend to rely on too small a sample of historical precedents."[46]

Partial Guard against Pitfall

Tasks 16-18 partially guard against this pitfall because they cause the computer application to automatically update the body of evidence monthly in the trend analysis matrices. In tasks 16-18 the computer automatically captures the Indicator Warning Levels, Target Warning Levels, and Country Warning Levels at the end of each month and plots them on trend analysis graphs (as shown in figures 1.14, 1.15, and 1.16 respectively). The graphs also show attempted and successful terrorist attacks. Additionally, the tasks require analysts to study and comment on the new evidence added to the trend analysis to determine whether they think any scales in the methodology for determining warning levels should be adjusted. The trend analysis templates remind analysts that successful terrorist attacks are not the only source of useful reference events; thwarted terrorist attacks also provide useful reference evidence because the terrorists still carried out their preparations for the attack despite the fact that it did not take place. The trend analysis tasks capitalize on that source of evidence by identifying when high warning levels corresponded to thwarted terrorist attacks. Thus analysts are actively and continuously adding to their body of evidence, which makes it a larger, more representative sample. This, however, is only a partial guard against the pitfall because: 1) the trend analysis tasks do not immediately provide analysts with the large sample of evidence they need, and 2) a limited number of reference events will likely continue in terrorism. (Of course, a limited number of terrorist attacks is a good thing, and thus the positive side of a limited sample in counterterrorism.)

21. The Anchoring and Adjustment Heuristic

Description of Pitfall

A process in which analysts resist changing their opinion by treating their opinion as tied to an anchor. The analysts tend base their estimates on familiar positions or "anchors." For example, "If asked whether the population of Turkey was greater or less than 30 million, you might give one or the other answer. If then asked what you thought the actual population was, you would very likely guess somewhere around 30 million, because you have been anchored by the previous answer." When the analysts receive contradictory evidence, they merely adjust their assessment to a value relatively close to the anchor.[47] The end result is that the assessment "fails to do justice to the importance of [the] additional information."[48]

Guard against Pitfall

Tasks 8-15 guard against this pitfall. Analysts face an anchoring and adjustment situation in task 10 when they are required to answer questions in the Indicator Key, Questions, Answers, & Evidence Logs. In these logs, analysts answer questions about an indicator's activity on a 5-level scale of: 1) "Almost Certainly True (~90%)," about 90 percent probability, color coded red on the website, 2) "Probably True (~70%)," color coded orange, 3) "Probably Not True (~30%)," color coded yellow, 4) "Almost Certainly Not True (~10%)," color coded gray, or 5) "Unknown (or ~)," color coded black. Whichever answer is already marked is likely to become the analyst's anchor. However, as explained in pitfall 7, tasks 8-15 protect against analysts *discounting* the significance of information on an assessment.

Moreover, tasks 10-15 also guard against this pitfall because they use automatic computer calculations that deny analysts the opportunity to hold back changes to all the other warning levels in the methodology with the anchoring and adjustment process. After analysts update their answers to the questions in the Indicator Key, Questions, Answers, & Evidence Logs, the computer program uses those answers as the basis, in tasks 10-15, to automatically calculate *all* the other warning levels in the methodology—Indicator Activity Levels, Indicator Warning Levels, Terrorist Intention Warning Levels, Terrorist Capability Warning Levels, Target Vulnerability Warning Levels, Target Risk Warning Levels, and Country Risk Warning Levels. Thus, for instance, if new evidence arrived that warranted an increase in a Terrorist Intention Warning Level from "Minor (~30%)" to "Significant (~70%)," then an analyst's anchoring and adjustment tendency would likely prevent him from raising the warning level to "Significant (~70%)," but the computer calculation would not. Additionally, if analysts decide to overwrite a computer calculation, they are required to write a justification to be displayed on the website, which adds another layer to the guard against this pitfall.

22. Deception: A-Type

Description of Pitfall

Deception is providing "misleading or false information in order to achieve the element of surprise.... There are two types of deception: ambiguity increasing (A-type) and ambiguity decreasing (M-type). There are two ways of implementing deception: active (up-playing capabilities & intentions) and passive (down-playing capabilities and intensions)."[49]

In A-type deception, the adversary surrounds his incriminating activity with irrelevant information.[50] Egyptian diplomats employed this type of deception by making multiple trips all over the Middle East to distract Israel from their trips to Syria. Israel knew Egypt would seek Syrian cooperation prior to an attack, but the other trips across the Middle East made the purpose of the trip to Syria appear unclear.[51]

Guard against Pitfall

Tasks 6 and 7 guard against this pitfall because they use indicators as filters that: 1) allow the incriminating activities (that must and are likely to occur before an attack) to go into a hypothesis matrix under the appropriate indicators, and 2) filter out the irrelevant information (that need not occur before an attack) into the Miscellaneous Indicators within the hypothesis matrix. In task 6, analysts file all raw intelligence reports in the database under all the terrorist groups, countries, specific targets, indicators, and key questions that apply. Since indicators identify what must and what is likely to happen before a terrorist attack, the indicators catch the threatening signals. Then in task 7, the computer program automatically creates *Potential Target Hypothesis Matrix* web-pages [as shown in figure 1.5, Hypothesis Matrix: Indicator List View (with Link to Raw Reports Display)] and displays hyperlinks to the reports under the appropriate indicator(s) within the hypothesis matrices. The irrelevant signals are filed under the Miscellaneous Indicators, which the computer application does not factor into determining the hypothesis matrices' warning levels in tasks 11-15. Thus, despite the irrelevant information, the threatening information is not deterred from raising a hypothesis matrix's warning level.

23. Deception: M-Type

Description of Pitfall

The adversary builds analysts' focus on the wrong target.[52] This "may be more difficult than A-type deception because it requires time and carefully orchestrated resources to build a series of misleading false signals." [53]

No Guard against Pitfall

The methodology does not guard against this pitfall.

24. Deception: Active

Description of Pitfall

The adversary causes an object or situation to seem *threatening* when in reality the adversary does not have the intention and/or the capability to carry out the threat.[54]

No Guard against Pitfall

The methodology does not guard against this pitfall.

25. Deception: Passive (Also Known As "Creeping Normalcy" or "Desensitization")

Description of Pitfall

Measures designed to make an object or situation appear nonthreatening. To do this, the adversary could "produce [additional] signals that suggest a non threatening explanation," or repeat the threatening signals so often that they no longer appear significant/exceptional/threatening.[55] North Korea produced signals to suggest a nonthreatening explanation in 1950 by announcing false peace initiatives while mobilizing its military under the pretense of an exercise.[56] North Korea has also used the tactic of repeating threatening signals to make them appear less significant by mobilizing its military many times for exercises. This tactic of repeating threatening signals so often that they no longer appear significant is also called creeping normalcy or desensitization.[57] Both methods (creating false nonthreatening signals and repeating threatening signals) are designed to cause analysts to ignore the threatening signals.

Guard against Pitfall

Tasks 6, 7, and 10 guard against this pitfall. Tasks 6 and 7 guards against the nonthreatening signals because (as already explained in pitfall 22) these tasks use indicators as filters that: 1) allow the threatening activities (that must and are likely to occur before an attack) to go into a hypothesis matrix under the appropriate indicators, and 2) filterout the nonthreatening information (that need not occur before an attack) into the Miscellaneous Indicators within the hypothesis matrix. The computer application does not factor the Miscellaneous Indicators into the hypothesis matrices' warning levels in tasks 11-15. Thus, despite the nonthreatening information, the threatening information is not deterred from raising a hypothesis matrix's warning level.

Task 10 guards against the tactic of repeating threatening signals to make them appear less significant/exceptional/threatening. Since indicators are the bases for determining all the other warning levels, if analysts guard against this pitfall at the indicator assessment level, then they also guard against it at the hypothesis assessment warning levels. In task 10, the computer application calculates the warning levels for the *quantitative* indicators via Utility Matrix 2 (shown in figure 1.9). The range selected for the degree of variation in big "T" in Utility Matrix 2 (figure 1.9) is designed to flag a repeating number of suspicious incidents in the quantitative indicators over 12 months as a "Significant (~70%)" Indicator Activity Level. Thus, if terrorists were to conduct about 2 cases of surveillance every month for a year, the computer program would show that seemingly normal level of monthly activity as "Significant (~70%)."

In task 10, the computer application calculates the warning levels for the *qualitative* indicators from the average of analysts' answers to the questions in the Indicator Key Questions, Answers, and Evidence Logs. The questions in these logs require analysts to answer questions on whether certain activities have *occurred*. The first time an analyst receives evidence that the activity has occurred, he will likely answer the question accordingly. The next time he receives additional evidence of that activity, it serves as more recorded evidence that the activity has occurred, possibly even changing his answer for instance from "Probably True (~70%)" to "Almost Certainly True (~90%)." If he continues to receive additional reports on the activity and becomes inclined to change his answer to indicate that the activity has "Probably Not (~30%)" or "Almost Certainly Not (~10%)" occurred, then his mistake will be obvious and highlighted as a blatant error because the reports/evidence are displayed next to the questions and answers on the log webpage. Furthermore, the fact that the questions, answers, and evidence are available on a webpage for all other analysts to review provides for a system of checks and balances, which adds another layer to the guard against this pitfall.

26. Assessment Does Not Account for Defender's Ability to Protect against Attacker's Capability

Description of Pitfall

Analysts do not account for a defending force's ability to protect against an attacker's capability. "What should interest intelligence analysts is not the enemy's absolute capabilities for launching an attack but rather his relative ones as compared with their . . . own [friendly] capabilities for blocking that attack. . . . Few intelligence analysts, however, are in a position to evaluate both the enemy's and their own . . . capabilities."[58] Consequently, "in most surprise attacks since 1939 incorrect assessment of capabilities was a central factor in the ultimate failure to predict." [59] Technically, this pitfall is a failure to assess a defender's *vulnerability and combine it* with the assessment of the attacker's capability. Vulnerability represents a defending force's capability to protect against an attack.

Intelligence is traditionally restricted to assessing only enemy force information, not friendly force information, and that restriction is a primary cause of this pitfall. The U.S. Intelligence Community does have assets that assess friendly vulnerability, but these are *coun-terintelligence* assets, which differ from positive/traditional intelligence assets. Despite the counterintelligence, typical intelligence assessments only include information on enemy forces.

Guard against Pitfall

Tasks 13, 14, and 1 guard against this pitfall because they combine assessments on both target vulnerability and terrorist capability (and terrorist intentions) into a risk assessment. In task 13, analysts assess a target's Vulnerability Warning Level using the vulnerability indicators. In task 14 the computer application averages the Target Vulnerability Warning Level with the Terrorist Capability Warning Level and the Terrorist Intentions Warning Level to determine the Target Risk Warning Level. Thus, for example, if a friendly target is highly vulnerable, but the enemy is only moderately capable, then the Target Risk Warning level will be somewhere in-between, possibly at "Significant (~70%)" (depending on the Terrorist Intention Warning Level). Therefore, analysts represent/assess an enemy's relative capability as compared with a defender's capability in the Target Risk Warning Level.

Also noteworthy, is that U.S. counterintelligence teams assess the vulnerability of U.S. military and diplomatic facilities around the world and high value targets in the U.S. such as nuclear facilities. Those vulnerability assessments and other elements necessary to assess vulnerability are identified in the list of Vulnerability Indicators (shown in table 1.4). Furthermore, in task 1, experts validate those indicators annually.[60]

27. Assessment Does Not Account for a Target's Changing Circumstances

Description of Pitfall

Analysts do not account for changes in circumstances surrounding a target, which vary an enemy's capability to attack the target.[61]

Guard against Pitfall

Tasks 10, 13, and 14 guard against this pitfall because the Vulnerability Indicators (listed in table 1.4) enable analysts to account for changes in circumstances surrounding a target. For instance, if a decision maker changes the security posture/FPCON of a target, analysts can, in task 10, change the Indicator Warning Level for the *Security Posture/FPCON Indicator*. Additionally, if a country reduces its cooperation with the U.S. on counterterrorism efforts, analysts can change the Indicator Warning Level for the *Level of Country's Cooperation with the U.S. Indicator.* Then in task 13, the computer automatically uses the new Indicator Warning Level values to update the Target Vulnerability Warning Level, which also automatically changes the Target Risk Warning Level in task 14. Thus analysts account for a target's changing circumstances via the Vulnerability Indicators, and account for how those changes vary an enemy's capability against the target via the Target Risk Waning Level.

28. Failing to Account for Gaps in Intelligence Collection Coverage

Description of Pitfall

An analyst cannot see activity in an indicator because of a gap in intelligence collection coverage, so he assesses a warning level lower than it should be.[62] A gap in collection coverage exists when intelligence collectors cannot or are unlikely to collect on a certain indicator at a certain location. For instance, it would be difficult to detect surveillance of a building on an open public street in a metropolitan area—such as the World Trade Center prior to the February 26, 1993 terrorist bombing or the OPM-SANG building in downtown Riyadh, Saudi Arabia, prior to the November 13, 1995 terrorist bombing.

Guard against Pitfall

Task 10 guards against this pitfall because analysts "deactivate" indicators that are assessed as noncollectable. The deactivated indicators are not factored into the computer's warning level calculations in tasks 11-15. Thus, the absence of information in a noncollectable indicator does not unduly lower the overall warning level assessment of a target. If the analyst does happen to receive an indication in a deactivated indicator, he can reactivate it.

Assessment of
Phase V (Focus Collectors on Intelligence Gaps to Refine/Update Conclusions): Guard against 2 of 2 Common Pitfalls

29. Failing to Focus Intelligence Collection on Gaps in Intelligence

Description of Pitfall

The Intelligence Community increases intelligence collection without using analysis to focus collectors on gaps in intelligence, which results in excess noise and less accurate assessments. Research suggests "an intensified collection effort does not necessarily lead to better analysis and more accurate estimates; when the additional information contains a large portion of noise, the risks of [information overload] and another intelligence failure leading to surprise may even increase."[63] "After each significant intelligence failure, a major effort is begun to improve collection of data," but that collection can actually hinder warning if analysts do not focus those collection efforts.[64]

Guard against Pitfall

Tasks 3, 10, 19, 20, and 21 guard against this pitfall. In task 3, analysts create a preset list of questions/Collection Requests on each of the 68 Terrorism Indicators. (The indicators identify what must happen and what is likely to happen before a terrorist attack.) The questions identify the key factors terrorism experts have determined are necessary to assess the status of a given terrorism indicator. In task 10, analysts use the Indicator Key Questions, Answers, & Evidence Log webpages to monitor incoming raw intelligence reports and determine answers to the questions/Collection Requests on a 5-level scale of: 1) "Almost Certainly True (~90%)," about 90 percent probability, color coded red on the website, 2) "Probably True (~70%)," color coded orange, 3) "Probably Not True (~30%)," color coded yellow, 4) "Almost Certainly Not True (~10%)," color coded gray, or 5) "Unknown (or ~50%)," color coded black. The questions to which an analyst answers unknown are gaps in intelligence. Tasks 19, 20, and 21 focus collectors on the Intelligence Gaps by automatically displaying the questions answered unknown in the appropriate Indicator, Target, and Country Warning Narrative: What We Know, Think, & Need to Know webpages. That helps prevent intelligence collectors from collecting nonessential information, which minimizes the noise that can cause information overload and less accurate assessments. Additionally, these webpages provide intelligence collectors near-real-time updates on the Collection Requests. That minimizes time gaps between assessment updates that cause intelligence collectors to collect information they were not aware had been collected since the last assessment.

30. Focusing Intelligence Collection on Information that Supports Favorite Hypothesis

Description of Pitfall

Analysts tend to request intelligence collectors to obtain information that will support their favorite hypothesis. Furthermore, the analysts do not seek information to refute hypotheses, which is the more effective method to test hypotheses.[65]

Guard against Pitfall

Tasks 3, 8, 10, 19, 20, and 21 guard against this pitfall. In task 3, analysts create a preset list of questions/Collection Requests on each of the 68 Terrorism Indicators. (The indicators identify what must happen and what is likely to happen before a terrorist attack. The question sets identify the key factors terrorism experts have determined are necessary to assess the status of a given terrorism indicator.) *In task 8, the computer application automatically puts all the same question sets on each of the 68 Terrorism Indicators in every terrorism hypothesis matrix.* The indicator question sets are listed in the Indicator Key Questions, Answers, & Evidence Logs within the hypothesis matrices. In task 10, analysts use the Indicator Key Questions, Answers, & Evidence Logs to monitor incoming raw intelligence reports and determine answers to the questions/Collection Requests on a 5-level scale of: 1) "Almost Certainly True (~90%)," about 90 percent probability, color coded red on the website, 2) "Probably True (~70%)," color coded orange, 3) "Probably Not True (~30%)," color coded yellow, 4) "Almost Certainly Not True (~10%)," color coded gray, or 5) "Unknown (or ~50%)," color coded black. The questions to which an analyst answers unknown are gaps in intelligence. In tasks 19, 20, and 21 the computer application automatically displays the questions answered unknown in the appropriate Indicator, Target, and Country Warning Narrative: What We Know, Think, & Need to Know webpages. Thus all hypothesis matrices are monitored according to the same predetermined list of Collection Requests and the computer automatically forwards all unanswered Collection Requests to the appropriate Indicator, Target, and Country Warning Narrative: What We Know, Think, & Need to Know webpages, which guards against an analyst sending forward *only* the questions/Collection Requests on the hypothesis he favors.

Additionally, in task 10, analysts use the *Anti-Indicators* in each hypothesis matrix to monitor information and questions on the things that would *disprove* a terrorism hypothesis. In tasks 19, 20, and 21 the computer application also automatically forwards the Collection Requests on the Anti-Indicators to the appropriate Indicator, Target, and Country Warning Narrative: What We Know, Think, & Need to Know webpages. Thus, tasks 10 and 19-21 ensure analysts request information to refute a hypothesis.

Assessment of
Phase VI (Communicate Conclusions/Give Warning):
Guard against 7 of 12 Common Pitfalls;
Partial Guard against 2; No Guard against 3

31. Communication Not Convincing

Description of Pitfall

Analysts fail to convey warning because their communication is not convincing.[66] The number one cause of warning failure is due to decision makers ignoring intelligence.[67]

Guard against Pitfall

Tasks 7, 8, 10-18, and 22 guard against this pitfall. People are more likely to be persuaded when they can see and understand a reasoning process. As a warning expert explains, "because policy makers know that [even experienced] analysts, like most mortals, cannot foretell the future, they need, instead, to be persuaded by clear articulation of rationale and evidence. . . . Unless analysts can demonstrate why and how the likelihood of a given event is increasing . . . their words are of little use."[68] Therefore, analysts must do everything within their power to make a warning picture persuasive. With the intuitive technique alone, analysts cannot demonstrate the reasoning process that led to their assessment.[69] The webpages generated in tasks 7, 8, and 10-18 are designed to convey the structured reasoning technique behind each warning level via 3 primary types of color-coded warning picture views: 1) country list view, 2) target list view, and 3) indicator list view (of terrorist intentions, terrorist capability, or target vulnerability). With the click of a button, analysts can further take decision makers all the way down to the detailed indications contained in individual raw intelligence reports shown as supporting evidence in the *Indicator Key Questions, Answers, & Evidence Logs*. Additionally, the webpages provide definitions and trend analysis for each warning level. Furthermore, leading graphic interface experts have found that the most effective way to capitalize on "human perceptual skills [which] are remarkable, but largely underutilized by current graphical interfaces," is to show "overview first, [then] zoom and filter, and then details-on-demand."[70] The webpages of this methodology follow that design principle. In task 22, analysts further convey the reasoning process when they use the website displays to brief decision makers.

Surprisingly though, a clear logical presentation of information is not always enough to get a decision maker to trust an analytical product, as demonstrated prior to Saddam Hussein's August 1990 invasion of Kuwait:

> Indicators were assessed early and accurately. . . . Collection was honed and focused; coordination with the analytic community was constant; and policy officials were informed of our conclusions at each major stage in the development of the threat, personally as well as in writing. . . . [with] a standard warning chronology . . . tracing the development of events during the past year. . . . Nevertheless, the warning . . . was not taken seriously because U.S. officials talked with, and accepted the judgment of a number of leaders in the Middle East as well as the Soviet Union.[71]

In this case, the *decision makers trusted the opinion of foreign leaders over their own intelligence warning system*. Therefore the question arises: What more can analysts do to gain decision makers' trust in their assessments?

Research shows that the process by which people develop trust for a product follows these steps: "Frequency [leads] to awareness, awareness to familiarity, and familiarity to trust."[72] Thus the road to trust is based on frequency in exposure to a product. Tasks 10-15 of the methodology create consistent display formats for each type of warning level. Thus every time decision makers view assessments about various countries, targets, and indicators, decision makers see the same display format, which creates frequency in exposure to the methodology's warning assessment display format. Additionally, in task 22, analysts brief decision makers on new threats using the website, which further promotes frequency in exposure to the product format. Moreover, the fact that the decision maker learns that the information is available to him at any time on a website further promotes frequency of use, awareness, and familiarity in the product.

32. Communication Not Clear

Description of Pitfall

Assessment fails to persuade decision makers because the language is ambiguous. "Looking back over the last 4 and a half decades of intelligence analysis that produced the prominent failures, it is possible to identify a number of . . . . glib and empty phrases [that] often creep into intelligence writing."[73] For instance, "We cannot rule out that country or leader X will undertake a given action."[74] There are 2 key reasons that assessments end up with this ambiguous language. First is that "especially amid controversy, estimators will reach for extra ambiguities in the search for interagency unanimity."[75] Second is that "frequently the analyst's rule is not to speak too clearly and precisely about the future unless he has to. When the analyst is pressed to make his estimate concrete and clear, the rule is to lower ["water down"] its probability."[76]

Guard against Pitfall

Tasks 10-15 guard against this pitfall because analysts must settle on a warning level for every terrorism indicator, target, and country on a 5-level scale of unambiguous language— "Critical (~90%)" color coded red in the hypothesis matrix webpages; "Significant (~70%)," color coded orange; "Minor (~30%)" color coded yellow; "Slight (~10%)" color coded gray; and "Unknown (or ~50%)" color coded black. Although analysts may try to use ambiguous language in the narratives that accompany the color coded warning levels, that language does not alter the bottom line color-coded unambiguous phrases of Critical (~90%), Significant (~70%), Minor (~30%), Slight (~10%), or Unknown (or ~50%).

Additionally in task 10, analysts must choose 1 of the following unambiguous answers for each key question on an indicator: 1) "Almost Certainly True (~90%)," about 90 percent probability, color coded red on the website, 2) "Probably True (~70%)," color coded orange, 3) "Probably Not True (~30%)," color coded yellow, 4) "Almost Certainly Not True (~10%)," color coded gray, or 5) "Unknown (or ~50%)," color coded black. Moreover, when analysts write an Indicator Warning Narrative: What We Know, Think, & Need to Know in task 19, they must use the Indicator Key Questions, Answers, & Evidence Log as an outline, which further pushes analysts to use the unambiguous phrases—almost certainly (~90%), probably (~70%), probably not (~30%), almost certainly not (~10%), or unknown (or ~50%). Furthermore, the unambiguous language carries up to narrative assessments on targets and countries because the computer application automatically combines every Indicator Warning Narrative: What We Know, Think, & Need to Know to create a Target Warning Narrative: What We Know, Think, & Need to Know, and also automatically combines every Target Warning Narrative: What We Know, Think, & Need to Know to create a Country Warning Narrative: What We Know, Think, & Need to Know.

Moreover, analysts are pressed to make their estimates concrete and concise at a low intimidation level of merely answering a question on an indicator in an Indicator Key Questions, Answers, & Evidence Log, rather than the high intimidation level of determining a major threat scenario's warning level, such as Target Risk Warning Level or a Country Risk Warning Level. Therefore, the analyst is less likely to feel he is being pressured to estimate the future and consequently less likely to lower ["water down"] the probability of his assessment.

33. Communication Not Concise

Description of Pitfall

Analysts' communication is not concise, which causes a decision maker to miss the important points during the limited time he has to study/review the evidence and rationale.[77]

Guard against Pitfall

Tasks 7 and 10-15 guard against this pitfall because they provide warning-level assessments in *color-coded* tables (hypothesis matrices) for quick reference. Additionally, tasks 10-15 create these color-coded tables/hypothesis matrices *in linked webpage displays*, which are renowned for compacting information clearly—thus enabling decision makers to access and absorb different levels of warning information more quickly.

34. Communication Not Timely

Description of Pitfall

Slow production and dissemination of assessments causes analysts to communicate warning too late. The nature of warning demands timely assessment and response. Today, despite major technological advances, assessments can take a month to get written and published and disseminated, and they are outdated soon thereafter. [78] In the September 11, 2001 terrorist attack case, there was just 1 month between the attack and the Priority 1 indication of terrorist travel.[79]

Guard against Pitfall

Tasks 10-15 guard against this pitfall because they employ computer technology to automate recurring tasks, analytical judgments, and updates to webpage displays. That saves time by enabling analysts to update many warning levels and their corresponding webpage displays with a single data entry. For instance, if an analyst changes an answer in an Indicator Key Questions, Answers, & Evidence Log that causes a change to the Indicator Activity Level for a strategic (countrywide) Terrorist Intention Indicator, then the computer application automatically updates the Terrorist Intention Warning Level and Target Risk Warning Level for all the targets in that country. Additionally, since these warning levels are automatically posted on the webpages, decision makers (and intelligence collectors) can see the changes in near-real-time.

35. The Pitfall of the Warning Dilemma

Description of Pitfall

The Warning Dilemma can cause analysts to warn too late. The analysts' Warning Dilemma is whether to: 1) risk crying wolf by providing warning when they are less sure of a threat so they allow a decision maker sufficient time to take necessary precautions, or 2) risk warning too late because they want to wait to warn until they are more certain of a threat so they avoid crying wolf. Thus, the warning pitfall of the Warning Dilemma is that analysts warn too late for a decision maker to take action because their fear of crying wolf causes them to delay their warning until they are more certain of the threat.[80]

Guard against Pitfall

Task 10 guards against this pitfall for 2 reasons. First, analysts are not required to repeatedly face the warning dilemma for every threat scenario because the computer program automatically applies the analysts' 1-time decision of which "level of confidence" they desire to warn at—such as a 70 percent certainty—to all warning level calculations.[81] Second, analysts face the Warning Dilemma at a low intimidation level of merely answering a question on an indicator in an Indicator Key Questions, Answers, & Evidence Log, rather than the high intimidation level of determining a major-threat scenario's warning level, such as Target Risk Warning Level or a Country Risk Warning Level. Therefore, analysts are less likely to fear they will be crying wolf on a major threat scenario since they are merely answering questions on just 1 of the 68 Terrorism Indicators in an evidence log.

36. The Pitfall of the Warning Paradox

Description of Pitfall

The Warning Paradox can erode decision maker's trust in analysts. The Warning Paradox is that: if analysts give warning, decision makers will increase security and cause the aggressor to cancel, delay, or redirect the attack, which in turn will make the analysts appear wrong; but if analysts don't give warning, the aggressor will carry out the attack, and the analysts will still appear wrong. Thus, the warning pitfall of the Warning Paradox is that analysts accurately predict a threat, and a decision maker's consequent security response causes the aggressor to cancel, delay, or redirect the attack, which in turn makes the analysts' prediction appear incorrect and degrades the decision maker's confidence in the analysts' future assessments.[82]

Partial Guard against Pitfall

Tasks 16, 17, and 18 partially guard against this pitfall by creating trend analysis webpages that display a record of warning levels, attacks, and known thwarted attacks. This enables analysts to show decision makers successes in the system—when high warning levels corresponded to known thwarted terrorist operations. It also enables analysts to show decision makers that they are studying failures in the system. This, however, is only a partial guard. Although the record of successes may help to bolster decision maker's confidence in assessments, unrecognized success can still occur to degrade the decision makers' trust. Furthermore, if the proposed methodology improves analysts' warning accuracy and persuasiveness, there would likely be an increase in the number of thwarted terrorist operations. If they are unrecognized successes more often than they are recognized successes, then the ill effects of the Warning Paradox may actually increase.

37. "The Super Analyst"[83]

Description of Pitfall

The decision maker thinks he knows best when he looks at the information because he has more experience or more "valuable" experience in the subject area than the analyst. In other words, the decision maker favors his own opinion over the analyst's assessment. This kind of decision maker is called a "Super Analyst."[84]

Guard against Pitfall

Tasks 7 and 10-15 guard against this pitfall. They create webpages that enable the analyst to show the decision maker a systematic reasoning behind the analyst's assessment in the form of hypothesis testing, matrix logic, and question set guidance. Those near-scientific rationales enable analysts to show the Super Analyst that the assessment is based on sound logic rather than the intuition of a "less experienced" analyst.

38. Decision Maker Has Access to Other Information

Description of Pitfall

A decision maker ignores a warning because he believes he has access to additional key information that the analyst does not. Sometimes, a decision maker has access to unique information from a foreign colleague—information that may not exist in U.S. Intelligence Community reporting because it was not collected. Additionally, fractionalized distribution of information within the Intelligence Community has contributed to decision makers' impression that analysts may lack key information.[85]

Partial Guard against Pitfall

Tasks 5, 6, and 7 partially guard against this pitfall. In task 5, the requirement for all intelligence and law enforcement agencies to forward all their terrorism-related raw intelligence reports to an Intelligence Community Master Database helps to assure decision makers that all the raw reports are being consolidated. In task 6, analysts profile the reports in the Terrorism Forecasting Database, which enables the computer application, in task 7, to display hyperlinks to the reports on webpages according terrorist networks, countries, targets, and indicators, *and that enables decision makers and analysts to see when they are operating off the same set of information.* No report can be removed from the database or website display when it is discounted from analysts' assessments (the report can only be color coded instead), so decision makers and analysts can avert misunderstandings over whether analysts are aware of reports that have been excluded from their assessments. This however, is only a partial guard against this pitfall because tasks 5, 6, and 7 cannot consolidate and display information decision makers obtain from foreign colleagues that the U.S. Intelligence Community has not collected.

39. Assessment Does Not Support Decision Maker's Policy

Description of Pitfall

A decision maker ignores a warning because it calls for an action which conflicts with his policy interests.[86]

No Guard against Pitfall

The methodology does not guard against this pitfall.

40. Fear of Provocation

Description of Pitfall

A decision maker ignores a warning because it calls for an action that he fears could provoke the very threat about which analysts are warning, or something worse.[87]

No Guard against Pitfall

The methodology does not guard against this pitfall.

41. Decision Maker Bias

Description of Pitfall

A decision maker ignores a warning because of his bias.[88] As explained in pitfall 8, bias is "an inclination . . . that inhibits impartial judgment [of facts and information]." [89] Intelligence warning experts have identified numerous biases, which include but are not limited to: mirror imaging, overconfidence, group think, vividness, favor of causal explanation (popularity of conspiracy theories), and favoring perception of centralized direction.[90] Although the biases have different rationales, they have the same end result: misjudgment of facts and information.

This pitfall differs from an analyst's bias in the effect. An analyst's bias alters the assessment he builds. A decision maker's bias does not alter the assessment that an analyst builds; his bias alters his response to the analyst's assessment.

No Guard against Pitfall

The methodology does not guard against this pitfall. The guards in the methodology that compel analysts to *include* all relevant information in an assessment and weigh the information properly to build an accurate assessment do not compel decision makers to *accept* the information in the assessment.

42. Intelligence Products Not Focused on Warning

Description of Pitfall

Analysts become consumed with providing current intelligence products rather than developing in-depth analysis products geared toward forecasting. "The plethora of new US security concerns since the end of the Cold War, including terrorism, crime, narcotics, [and] humanitarian issues . . . has resulted in resources being stretched thin." This has decimated dedicated warning staffs in the Intelligence Community, who would conduct in-depth analytical forecasting. Analysts have become pressured to merely keep up with current intelligence, leaving little time for in-depth analytical forecasting. [91] "There is more current intelligence reporting and less attention to strategic warning."[92]

Guard against Pitfall

Tasks 6, 7, 10-18, and 23 guard against this pitfall because they make effective use of analysts' time by: 1) using automated technology to apply analysts' daily judgments on new intelligence to both current intelligence products and strategic warning products, and 2) automating necessary recurring tasks that build/update the strategic forecasting products.

In task 6, when analysts profile a report in the Terrorism Forecasting Database, if they check 1 of the boxes indicating a new target, a miscellaneous indicator, an urgent report (pertaining to a threat within the next 30 days), a threat status exists, a threat status is indeterminable, or an attack/attempted attack occurred, then the computer program automatically checks the box to enter the report into the Daily Readfile webpage (shown in figure 1.21). Then the computer program displays the report in both the Daily Readfile (a current intelligence product) shown in figure 1.21 in task 23, and the appropriate hypothesis matrix (a strategic warning product) shown in figure 1.5 in task 7. Thus the use of automated technology in tasks 6, 7, and 23 enables analysts' daily judgments on incoming raw intelligence reports to automatically apply to both current intelligence products and strategic warning products.

Tasks 10-18 automate necessary recurring tasks that build/update the strategic forecasting products. In task 10, after analysts use the incoming raw intelligence reports to answer questions in the Indicator Key, Questions, Answers, & Evidence Logs, the computer application, in tasks 10-15, uses those answers as the basis to automatically calculate *all* warning levels in the methodology—Indicator Activity Levels, Indicator Warning Levels, Terrorist Intention Warning Levels, Terrorist Capability Warning Levels, Target Vulnerability Warning Levels, Target Risk Warning Levels, and Country Risk Warning Levels. Additionally, tasks 16-18 automate the necessary recurring tasks that build each Indicator, Target, and Country Warning Narrative: What We Know, Think, & Need to Know webpage. After analysts use the Indicator Key, Questions, Answers, & Evidence Logs as outlines to create a narrative assessment on each indicator in task 16, the computer application automatically combines those Indicator Warning Narratives: What We Know, Think, & Need to Know into the appropriate Target Warning Narrative: What We Know, Think, & Need to Know in task 17. Then in task 18, the computer application automatically combines all the Target Warning Narratives related to a given country into a Country Warning Narrative: What We Know, Think, & Need to Know. Thus, to update a strategic warning narrative on a country or target, the analysts need only write an executive summary paragraph because the computer application has already synthesized their daily work on indicators into the body paragraphs of the narratives. Moreover, in tasks 16-18, the computer application also automatically displays all the questions to which analysts answered "Unknown (or ~50%)" (from the Indicator Key, Questions, Answers, & Evidence Logs) in the corresponding Indicator, Target, and Country Warning Narrative: What We Know, Think, & Need to Know webpages.

82 Percent Guard against Common Warning Pitfalls

Research shows that intelligence warning accuracy is about 30 percent, and some warning experts believe that 30 percent is probably about the best forecasting can be for interactive human decision-making events,[93] such as terrorism. However, if some common past mistakes are not repeated, then there is a chance to improve accuracy. Out of 42 common warning pitfalls, 33 guards and 3 partial guards is an 82 percent overall guard against the pitfalls (counting each partial guard as a half percentage point.) If each pitfall occurred equally often, then this methodology could potentially provide about a 52 percent increase in warning accuracy. However, it is likely that certain pitfalls occur more often than others, and it is possible that 1 or more of the nonguarded (or guarded) pitfalls occurs significantly more often than others. That would significantly lower (or raise) the methodology's potential for accuracy. Furthermore, Chaos Theory brings other complicating elements into play. Nonetheless, even if the improvement is closer to just 10 percent, preventing just 1 additional terrorist attack will save lives.

Notes

1. This research identified 42 pitfalls; there may be more. Please advise the author of any additional pitfalls.

2. CDR Steven Carey, USN, "Strategic Warning and Threat Management," lecture presented in ANA680 class at the Joint Military Intelligence College (JMIC), Washington, D.C., February 2002; Richard K. Betts, *Surprise Attack: Lessons for Defense Planning* (Washington, D.C.: The Brookings Institution, 1982); John Hughes-Wilson, *Military Intelligence Blunders* (London: Robinson Publishing, Ltd., 1999); Kam; James Miskel, "Are we learning the Right Lessons from Africa's humanitarian Crises?" *Naval War College Review* 111, no. 3 (Summer 1999):137-45; Gregory F. Treverton and James Klocke, "The Fall of the Shah of Iran," *C16-88-794.0*, Kennedy School of Government (Cambridge, MA: President and Fellows of Harvard College Copyright, 1988).

3. McDevitt, "Summary of Indicator-Based-Methodology."

4. Russo, 120.

5. Russo, 14.

6. Kam, 102, 106.

7. Russo, 135.

8. JMIC "Strategic Warning" course.

9. Russo, 130.

10. JMIC "Strategic Warning" course.

11. Shneiderman, "The Eyes Have It."

12. Kam, 53.

13. Kam, 97.

14. Kam, 97.

15. Kam, 97.

16. Richard K. Betts, *Surprise Attack: Lessons for Defense Planning* (Washington, D.C.: The Brookings Institution, 1982), 43. Cited hereafter as Betts.

17. JMIC "Strategic Warning" course.

18. Kam, 95-96, 138.

19. Kam, 138.

20. *Dictionary.Com*, www.dictionary.com (30 May 2002). Cited hereafter as *Dictionary.Com*.

21. JMIC "Strategic Warning" course.

22. McDevitt, "Summary of Indicator-Based-Methodology."

23. Kam, 103-104; JMIC "Strategic Warning" course.

24. Kam, 103.

25. Kam, 104; JMIC "Strategic Warning" course.

26. Kam, 103.

27. Kam, 104-105; JMIC "Strategic Warning" course.

28. Kam, 103.

29. Kam, 103; JMIC "Strategic Warning" course.

30. Kam, 103.

31. Kam, 103.

32. Russo, 14.

33. Kam, 106.

34. Kam, 49, 97.

35. Kam, 122.

36. Kam, 123-124.

37. JMIC "Strategic Warning" course.

38. Kam, 138; JMIC "Strategic Warning" course.

39. Kam, 91, 137.

40. JMIC "Strategic Warning" course.

41. Kam, 91.

42. Steven R. Mann, "Chaos Theory and Strategic Thought," *Parameters* (Autumn 1992): 54-67; JMIC "Strategic Warning" course.

43. Kam, 106-107.

44. Kam, 107.

45. Kam, 107.

46. Kam, 110.

47. JMIC "Strategic Warning" course; "Anchoring and Adjustment Heuristic," *Changing Minds.org* 2004, http://changingminds.org/explanations/theories/anchoring_adjustment.htm (20 Feb 2004).

48. Kam, 111.

49. Jan Goldman, *Words of Warning: A Glossary for Strategic Warning and Threat Management, Second Edition* (Washington, D.C.: Joint Military Intelligence College, 1996), 40. Cited hereafter as *Words of Warning.*

50. *Intelligence Warning Terminology*, 5; JMIC "Strategic Warning" course; Kam, 48.

51. John Hughes-Wilson, *Military Intelligence Blunders* (London: Robinson Publishing, Ltd., 1999), 238. Cited hereafter as Hughes-Wilson.

52. *Intelligence Warning Terminology*, 28; JMIC "Strategic Warning" course; *Words of Warning*, 26.

53. *Intelligence Warning Terminology*, 26.

54. *Intelligence Warning Terminology*, 6; JMIC "Strategic Warning" course.

55. *Intelligence Warning Terminology*, 28; Kam, 144; JMIC "Strategic Warning" course.

56. Betts, 54-55.

57. JMIC "Strategic Warning" course; *Intelligence Warning Terminology*, 11.

58. Kam, 73.

59. Kam, 72.

60. The author is aware that there are more indicators of target vulnerability than listed in table 1.4, but has not listed them because they are accounted for in the Facility Vulnerability Assessment (VA) Indicator. Counterintelligence agencies write Facility Vulnerability Assessments (VAs), which assess facilities according to those indicators.

61. Kam, 73.

62. Kam, 47, 49.

63. Kam, 55.

64. Kam, 53, 55.

65. Kam, 137.

66. Kam, 24-29, 168; JMIC "Strategic Warning" course.

67. Garst, 7; Heymann, 55.

68. McCarthy, 24.

69. *Dictionary.Com* (30 May 2002); Folker, 5.

70. Dr. Ben Shneiderman, Professor of Computer Science and the University of Maryland, Abstract to the National Security Agency, subject: "The Eyes Have It: User Interfaces for Information Visualization," 3 April 2002, attachment to e-mail from David T. Moore, NSA, Analyst, MD to author, 3 April 2002.

71. Allen, 43.

72. Seth Godin, "Applying Old Marketing Rules to the Cyber World," *Business Week Book Excerpt, Business Week Online* 1999, www.businessweek.com/smallbiz/news/coladvice/book/bk990709.htm (30 May 2002). Cited hereafter as Godin, "Applying Old Marketing Rules to the Cyber World."

73. McCarthy, 25.

74. McCarthy, 27.

75. Kam, 28, 168.

76. Kam, 28.

77. JMIC "Strategic Warning" course.

78. JMIC "Strategic Warning" course.

79. "CNN Presents: Investigating Terror," on CNN, produced by CNN, October 2001; William Matthews, "In the System: Do commercial firms have the data needed to fight terrorism?" *Federal Computer Week*, 11 January 2002, 24.

80. JMIC "Strategic Warning" course.

81. Russo, 96.

82. *Intelligence Warning Terminology*, 40; JMIC "Strategic Warning" course.

83. JMIC "Strategic Warning" course.

84. JMIC "Strategic Warning" course.

85. JMIC "Strategic Warning" course.

86. JMIC "Strategic Warning" course.

87. JMIC "Strategic Warning" course.

88. JMIC "Strategic Warning" course.

89. *Dictionary.Com* (30 May 2002).

90. JMIC "Strategic Warning" course.

91. Robert D. Vickers Jr., "The Mission to Warn: Disaster Looms," *Defense Intelligence Journal,* no. 7 (Fall 1998): 11-12. Cited hereafter as Vickers.

92. Vickers, 12.

93. Garst, 6.

Chapter 3

How to Make It Happen:
Recommendations for Implementation

*Why do projects fail? . . . Few information systems projects fail for technical reasons.
Most projects fail because they are not effectively managed and the most important and
complex aspect of the management task is managing relationships with the people involved.*
Joint Information Systems Committee, www.jiscinfonet.ac.uk/InfoKits/project-
management/pm-intro-1.2

This final chapter proposes 6 ideal-world recommendations to effectively implement the proposed
forecasting system—5 of which the Intelligence Community controls and 1 that policy makers
control. The author recommends these measures because policy makers have announced that they
are seeking such recommendations.

As part of a series of initiatives to improve coordination and communication among all levels of
government and the American public in the fight against terrorism, President Bush signed Homeland Security Presidential Directive 3, creating the Homeland Security Advisory System (HSAS).
The advisory system will be the foundation for building a comprehensive and effective communi-
cations structure for the dissemination of information regarding the risk of terrorist attacks to all
levels of government and the American people.

The Attorney General will be responsible for developing, implementing and managing the system.
In conjunction with the development of this new system, the Attorney General will open a 45-day
comment period in order to seek the views of officials at all levels of government, law enforcement
and the American public. Ninety days after the conclusion of the comment period, the Attorney
General in coordination with the Director of the Office of Homeland Security—will present a final
Homeland Security Advisory System to the President for approval.[1]

For this methodology to fulfill its potential of guarding against 82 percent of 42 common
warning pitfalls, the author recommends the following 6 measures that correspond to the 6 phases
of Indications & Warning.

1. Validate the Indicators and Develop Indicator Question Sets

The leading counterterrorism community experts should meet to: 1) validate the list of 68 Terrorism Indicators (shown in table 1.4), and 2) develop the corresponding indicator question sets. The experts should validate the indicators for the 3 components of terrorism risk—terrorist intentions, terrorist capability, and target vulnerability. Although this author systematically reviewed evidence from case studies of terrorist operations, raw intelligence reporting, the Al Qaeda Manual, and interviews and surveys of terrorism analysts, the author was unable to tap as many terrorism experts as desired. Additionally, the question sets for the 61 *qualitative* Terrorism Indicators still need to be developed. Meeting with the terrorism experts and conducting the research necessary to develop these question sets would likely be a 4-month project for a team of researchers.

2. A New Law, Presidential Directive, or DCI Instruction

Someone with power needs to establish the requirement that all fifteen Member Organizations of the Intelligence Community and other U.S. federal organizations that may have terrorism-related information forward *all* their raw intelligence reports (on all intelligence topics, not just terrorism) to an Intelligence Community Master Database. Additionally, the FBI should be instructed to consolidate suspicious incident reports from local law enforcement agencies, private security companies, commercial firms, and private citizens to forward to the database. This would enable terrorism forecasting analysts to easily and efficiently draw all the terrorism-related reporting from a single Intelligence Community database into a terrorism forecasting-specific database that profiles each raw report according to the terrorism forecasting-specific data profile elements identified in this methodology. Today, terrorism analysts would have to gain access to at least 6 different databases to get all terrorism-related raw intelligence reporting. There is currently no database in the Intelligence Community that consolidates all the raw intelligence reporting from all the Intelligence Community Member Organizations. Fractionalized distribution of information was cited as a key cause of warning failure in 2 of the U.S.'s most devastating surprise attacks—Pearl Harbor and the September 11 terrorist attacks.[2] Understandably there is a need to compartmentalize some information in order to protect sensitive sources and methods. Today's Information Technology is capable of restricting access within a database based on both a report's classification and a user's identification. The major benefit of hindsight after intelligence warning failures is that it is the first time all the information has been consolidated. Of course analysts need all available pieces of a puzzle to make the best possible assessment.

3. Train Analysts on the Operation and Rationale behind the Hypothesis Matrices, and Validate the Display Design

Raw Reporting Profilers, Indicator Specialists, and Senior Warning Officers should be trained on the rationale behind the hypothesis matrix displays. Analysts should understand that the reports are displayed in the hypothesis matrices because analysis of competing hypotheses is 1 of the most effective techniques for determining the scale of a threat.[3] Analysts should understand that every time a report arrives that relates to a target or terrorist group not listed in the database, Raw Reporting Profilers are required to add the new target or terrorist group to the list, which causes the database to create a new hypothesis matrix on the website display. The training should emphasize that no raw intelligence report is ever removed from a hypothesis matrix, that there are only 5 valid reasons to discount (not remove) a raw report, and that a color-coding system identifies discounted reports. Analysts should understand that these guidelines are critical to ensuring the threat picture/hypothesis matrices show ground truth.

Furthermore, analysts should review the design of the hypothesis matrices to ensure they display information in the most succinct, clear, and persuasive way possible. The display format should follow the design principle that graphic interface experts have learned is the most effective way to capitalize on human perceptual skills—"Overview first, [then] zoom and filter, and then details-on-demand."[4] Poor sorting and display of information can be the fundamental cause of problems with drawing conclusions, the next phase of I&W/forecasting.

4. Appoint and Train Analysts, Validate the Systematic Process, and Develop the Software

Someone with power needs to appoint the staff necessary to operate the methodology—84 Raw Reporting Profilers, 18 Indicator Specialists, and 5 Senior Warning Officers. Again, that staff, 107 analysts, is far less than the Intelligence Community currently has working to provide worldwide terrorism Indications & Warning assessments. This system is a highly efficient use of personnel resources because recurring analytical tasks have been automated wherever possible, and the analysts are working in a coordinated systematic effort. The analysts should also be trained on their roles in operating the methodology as described in the Staffing Plan for this methodology.

Additionally, analysts should validate the systematic process by: 1) reviewing more case-study evidence to validate the scales for big "T" and little "t;" 2) researching and incorporating additional structured techniques if appropriate; and 3) reviewing and validating the logic and assumptions of the methodology.

There's also a technical development that is necessary. None of the webpages on the CD interact with a database as described. Nor has a database been built according to the proposed design that can make the automated calculations described. Developing these webpage templates and the corresponding database design would likely take 4 months depending on how many people are working on it and their level of expertise. FBI contractors estimated 3 months and $250,000 if 4 expert developers were working on it full time.

5. Train Analysts on Generating Collection Requests and Publish Revised Collection Plan for Terrorism Forecasting

Indicator Specialists and Senior Warning Officers should be trained on how to generate Collection Requests on gaps in intelligence. The training should emphasize that: 1) Collection Requests on a given Terrorism Indicator should be applied/generated for every terrorism hypothesis matrix (this is automated) to guard against the warning pitfall of seeking evidence to confirm a favorite hypothesis, and 2) Collection Requests should be geared toward disproving (rather than proving) a hypothesis, which is 2 times more effective in hypothesis testing. Additionally, the 68 Terrorism Indicators and corresponding question sets should be used to publish a revised Collection Plan for terrorism forecasting.

6. Brief Decision Makers on Their New Forecasting System

A Senior Warning Officer should use the website display to brief decision makers on their new forecasting/warning system. This explanation will show decision makers that the website display conveys the reason process and supporting evidence/raw intelligence reports behind each warning level. This explanation will also begin the process of familiarization that research shows leads to trust. "Frequency [leads] to awareness, awareness to familiarity, and familiarity to trust."[5] Since the number 1 cause of warning failure is decision makers ignoring intelligence, analysts must do everything within their power to make warning persuasive.

Website Templates Using Tested and Proven Analytical Techniques Improve the Terrorism Forecasting Process

Rather than face the War on Terrorism with the traditional intuition-dominated approach, this methodology offers a systematic forecasting tool that guards against 82 percent of common warning pitfalls, and ultimately, improves the terrorism forecasting/warning process. The website conveys the reasoning process behind each warning level. The use of automated technology saves time and manpower and ensures accuracy in calculations, immediate updates, and consistency in the necessary, recurring judgments. Analysts guide collectors, and collectors update analysts in near-real-time. This system fuses interagency intelligence into a meaningful terrorism warning picture while still allowing for the compartmenting necessary to protect sensitive sources and methods. The enclosed CD is the tool to implement this terrorism forecasting system. The website on the CD forms a purposeful, focused tool to analyze the terrorist target, and most importantly, in near-real-time, turns raw information into actionable intelligence that can save lives.

Notes

1. "Gov. Ridge Announces Homeland Security Advisory System," *Presidential News and Speeches, The Whitehouse Homepage* 2002, www.whitehouse.gov/news/releases/2002/03/20020312-1.html (29 Apr. 2002). The author became aware of this solicitation 1 day after the close of the comment period and immediately submitted this proposal with approval from the point of contact.

2. Hughes-Wilson, 76.

3. McCarthy, 21.

4. Shneiderman, "The Eyes Have It."

5. Godin, "Applying Old Marketing Rules to the Cyber World."

Bibliography

A source, mid-level intelligence professional at a national intelligence organization, who wishes to remain anonymous. Interview by author, 10 July 2002.

Allen, Charles E. "Warning and Iraq's Invasion of Kuwait: A Retrospective Look." *Defense Intelligence Journal* 7, no. 2 (Fall 1998): 33-44.

"Al Qaeda Manual." *United States Department of Justice.* www.usdoj.gov/ag/trainingmanual.htm (21 Apr. 2002).

"Anchoring and Adjustment Heuristic," *Changing Minds.org.* 2004. http://changing-minds.org/explanations/theories/anchoring_adjustment.htm (20 Feb 2004).

Betts, Richard K. *Surprise Attack: Lessons for Defense Planning.* Washington, D.C.: The Brookings Institution, 1982.

Carey, Steven, CDR, USN. "Strategic Warning and Threat Management." Lecture presented in ANA680 class at the Joint Military Intelligence College. Washington, D.C., February 2002.

"CNN Presents: Investigating Terror." On CNN. Produced by CNN, October 2001.

"CNN Saturday Morning News, Interview With John Carroll." *CNN.* www.cnn.com. Aired 20 October 2001, under the "Transcripts" link (6 Jun. 2002).

Colin Powell on I&W: Address to the Department of Defense Warning Working Group. Distributed by the Joint Military Intelligence College, Washington, D.C. 1991. Videocassette.

"Counterdrug Intelligence Analysis." Lecture presented in CDIAC class at the Joint Military Intelligence Training Center. Washington, D.C., August 2002.

Crystal Square Apartments Management. Subject: "Building Security Advisory for Real Estate Owners and Managers of Residential Property: FBI General Threat Information for Residential Property Owners/Managers." 20 May 2002.

Dictionary.Com. www.dictionary.com (30 May 2002).

Facer, Tom, USN. Instructor at the Joint Military Intelligence Training Center, Defense Intelligence Agency. Interview by the author, 2 September 2002.

Federal Bureau of Investigation (FBI). *Terrorism in the United States 1998.* Washington D.C.: FBI, 1998.

Folker, Robert D. Jr., MSgt, USAF. *Intelligence Analysis in Theater Joint Intelligence Centers: An Experiment in Applying Structured Methods.* Joint Military Intelligence College Occasional Paper, no. 7. Washington, D.C.: Joint Military Intelligence College, January 2000.

Garst, Ronald D. "Fundamentals of Intelligence Analysis." 5-7 in *Intelligence Analysis ANA 630,* no. 1, edited by Joint Military Intelligence College. Washington, D.C.: Joint Military Intelligence College, 2000.

Godin, Seth. "Applying Old Marketing Rules to the Cyber World." *Business Week Book Excerpt, Business Week Online.* 1999. www.businessweek.com/smallbiz/news/coladvice/book/bk990709.htm (30 May 2002).

Goldman, Jan. *Intelligence Warning Terminology.* Washington, D.C.: Joint Military Intelligence

College, 2001.

_____. *Words of Warning: A Glossary for Strategic Warning and Threat Management, Second Edition.* Washington, D.C.: Joint Military Intelligence College, 1996.

"Gov. Ridge Announces Homeland Security Advisory System." *Presidential News and Speeches, The Whitehouse Homepage.* 2002. www.whitehouse.gov/news/releases/2002/03/20020312-1.html (29 Apr. 2002).

Heymann, Hans, Jr. "The Intelligence—Policy Relationship." 53-62 in *Intelligence Analysis ANA 630,* no. 1, edited by Joint Military Intelligence College. Washington, D.C.: Joint Military Intelligence College, 2000.

Hooper, Steve. Special Agent, Counterterrorism Division, Federal Bureau of Investigation (FBI). Interview by the author, 12 February 2002.

Hughes-Wilson, John. *Military Intelligence Blunders.* London, UK: Robinson Publishing, Ltd., 1999.

Interagency OPSEC Support Staff. "Operations Security (OPSEC)." *Employees' Guide to Security Responsibilities.* http://rf-web.tamu.edu/files/SECGUIDE/S2unclas/Opsec.htm (5 Jun. 2002).

Joint Information Systems Committee (JISC). "Project Management/Introduction: 1.2 Why do Projects Fail?" *JISC infoNet.* 2004. www.jiscinfonet.ac.uk/InfoKits/project-management/pm-intro-1.2 (23 Feb. 2004).

Jones, Morgan D. *The Thinker's Tool Kit: Fourteen Skills for Making Smarter Decisions in Business and in Life.* New York: Random House, 1995.

Kam, Ephraim. *Surprise Attack: The Victim's Perspective.* Cambridge, MA: Harvard University Press, 1988.

Kauppi, Mark V. "Counterterrorism Analysis." *Defense Intelligence Journal* 11, no. 1 (Winter 2002): 39-53.

Keith, Leon Drouin. "Calif. Bridge Subject of Alert." *South Coast Today.* I November 2002. www.s-t.com/daily/11-01/11-02-01/a01wn006.htm (19 Jul. 2002).

Kessler, Ronald. *The FBI.* New York: Pocket Books, 1993.

Laudon, Kenneth C., and Jane P. Laudon. *Management Information Systems: Organization and Technology in Network Enterprise, 4th ed.* Upper Saddle River, NJ: Prentice-Hall, Inc., 2001.

Lewis, Niel A. "F.B.I. Chief Admits 9/11 Might Have Been Detectable." *New York Times,* 30 May 2002. *The New York Times on the Web* (31 May 2002).

Mann, Steven R. "Chaos Theory and Strategic Thought." *Parameters* (Autumn 1992): 54-67.

"Making Intelligence Smarter: The Future of U.S. Intelligence." *Report of an Independent Task Force.* 1996. www.copi.com/articles/intelrpt/cfr.html (23 Jul. 1999).

Matthews, William. "In the System: Do Commercial Firms Have the Data Needed to Fight Terrorism?" *Federal Computer Week.* 11 January 2002, 20-26.

McCarthy, Mary O. "The Mission to Warn: Disaster Looms." *Defense Intelligence Journal* 7, no. 2 (Fall 1998): 17-31.

McDevitt, James J. *Summary of Indicator-Based-Methodology.* Unpublished handout, n.p., n.d. Provided in January 2002 at the Joint Military Intelligence College.

"Members of the Intelligence Community (IC)." *United States Intelligence Community—Who We Are.* 9 November 2003. www.intelligence.gov/1-members.shtml (2 February 2004).

Miller, Judith, and Don Van Natta Jr. "White House Asked F.B.I. about Unreported Threats." *New York Times,* 23 May 2002.

Miskel, James. "Are We Learning the Right Lessons from Africa's Humanitarian Crises?" *Naval War College Review* 111, no. 3 (Summer 1999): 137-45.

National Warning Staff, DCI Warning Committee. "National Warning System." Handout provided in January 2002 at the Joint Military Intelligence College.

O'Leary, Jeffery, Major, USAF. "Surprise and Intelligence: Towards a Clearer Understanding." *Air Power Journal,* (Spring 1994).

Potts, Michael. Special Agent, Counterterrorism Division, FBI. Interview by the author, 12 February 2002.

Russo, J. Edward, and Paul J. H. Schoemaker. *Decision Traps: The Ten Barriers to Brilliant Decision-Making and How to Overcome Them.* New York: Rockefeller Center, 1989.

Shneiderman, Ben, PhD. Professor of Computer Science at the University of Maryland. Abstract to the National Security Agency. Subject: "The Eyes Have It: User Interfaces for Information Visualization." 3 April 2002. Attachment to e-mail from David T. Moore, NSA, Analyst, MD to author, 3 April 2002.

Survey. "Prioritization of Terrorism Indicator Categories." Conducted by the author, January 2002.

Treverton, Gregory F., and James Klocke, "The Fall of the Shah of Iran," *C16-88-794.0*, Kennedy School of Government. Cambridge, MA: President and Fellows of Harvard College Copyright, 1988, 1-19.

Trochim, William M. K. "Qualitative Data." *Cornell University: Research Methods Knowledge Base.* 2002. http://trochim.human.cornell.edu/kb/qualdata.htm (31 May 2002).

_____. "The Qualitative Debate." *Cornell University: Research Methods Knowledge Base.* 2002. http://trochim.human.cornell.edu/kb/qualdeb.htm (31 May 2002).

"Unified Command Plan 2002 (UCP 02)." *Proposed EUCOM Area of Responsibility Change (AOR).* 1 October 2002. *United States European Command,* www.eucom.mil/AOR/index.htm (12 June 2002).

United States Department of State. *Patterns of Global Terrorism 1998.* Washington, D.C.: Office of the Secretary of State, 1999.

_____. *Patterns of Global Terrorism 2000.* Washington, D.C.: Office of the Secretary of State, 2001.

Vickers, Robert D. Jr. "The Mission to Warn: Disaster Looms." *Defense Intelligence Journal,* no. 7 (Fall 1998): 9-15.

Whetstone, Doug. "Building an Attack Template." Briefing presented at the FBI. Washington, D.C., November 2002.

Whitaker, Robert L., Major, USAF. Instructor, Joint Military Intelligence College, Washington, D.C. Attachment to e-mail from Major Robert L. Whitaker, USAF, Instructor, Joint Military Intelligence College, Washington, D.C., to author, 10 July 2002.

Index

42, 45, 47, 53, 63, 64, 66, 67, 70, 72,
   73, 79, 80, 81, 82, 83, 84
Indicator List View (hypothesis matrix in
   forecasting website), 5, 19-20, 23, 24,
   25, 29, 30-31, 33, 35, 38, 42, 47, 64, 73,
   74, 76, 81
indicator priority, 11, 13-14, 21, 29, 35, 45,
   54-55, 72, 83
Indicator Specialist, 8, 28, 33, 45, 51, 52-55,
   56, 57, 92, 93
Indicator Warning Level, 9, 28-36, 37, 38,
   39, 42, 46, 70, 72, 74, 75, 78, 87
*Indicator Warning Narrative: What We
   Know, Think, & Need to Know,* 9, 42,
   45, 53, 82
Information Feasibility/Viability, 23, 24, 25,
   26, 27, 67
Information Validity, 23-27, 28, 29, 33, 49
intelligence collector. *See* collector (of intelligence)
Intelligence Community, 1-3, 7, 10, 16-18,
   47, 48, 51, 57, 64, 65, 66-67, 79, 85, 86,
   91, 92, 93
Intelligence Community Master Database, 7,
   17-19, 65, 92
Intelligence Gaps, 7, 9, 24, 28, 35, 45, 46,
   47, 61, 62, 78-80, 93
Intentions (of adversary), 10, 11, 13, 18, 19,
   36, 39, 47, 64, 73, 78, 81, 92. *See also*
   risk (components of); Terrorist Intention Indicators; Terrorist Intention
   Warning Level
intuition, 2-3, 12, 27, 47, 63, 85

key questions (for indicator), 9, 14-16, 17,
   18, 21-22, 35, 45, 52, 67, 69, 72, 76, 82.
   *See also Indicator Key Questions, An-
   swers, & Evidence Log*
key question set (for indicator). *See* key
   questions (for indicator)

law enforcement, 10, 11-12, 17, 65, 85, 91,
   92

"M," 30, 31, 32, 33, 53
Miscellaneous Indicators, 12-13, 33, 37, 38,
   39, 53, 57, 63, 65-66, 73, 75-76, 77. *See
   also* indicator (definition of)

NRIS. *See* Nuclear & Radiological Indicator
   Specialist
Nuclear & Radiological Indicator Specialist
   (NRIS), 53, 54, 55, 56

phase I (of terrorism forecasting methodology), 7, 8, 9, 10-16, 61, 62, 63
phase II (of terrorism forecasting methodology), 7, 8, 9, 16-17, 61, 62, 63
phase III (of terrorism forecasting methodology), 7, 8, 9, 17-27, 61, 62, 63
phase IV (of terrorism forecasting methodology), 7, 8, 9, 28-44, 61, 62, 63
phase V (of terrorism forecasting methodology), 7, 8, 9, 45-47, 61, 62, 63
phase VI (of terrorism forecasting methodology), 7, 8, 9, 47-50, 61, 62, 63
priority (of indicator). *See* indicator priority

qualitative information/indicators, 2, 11-12,
   28, 52, 77, 92
quantitative information/indicators, 12, 30,
   53, 77

raw intelligence report, 9, 10, 13, 16-27, 33,
   45, 47, 49-50, 51, 52, 53, 56, 57, 92;
   and common warning pitfalls, 63, 64,
   65, 66, 67, 71, 72, 73, 74, 76, 79, 80,
   81, 85, 87
raw report. *See* raw intelligence report
Raw Reporting Profiler (RRP), 8,18, 51, 52,
   56, 57, 92, 93
risk (components of), 10, 11, 36, 37, 39, 64,
   92. *See also* Country Risk Warning
   Level; Target Risk Warning Level
RRP. *See* Raw Reporting Profiler

Senior Warning Officer (SWO), 8, 35, 42,
   43, 44, 46, 47, 51, 53, 56-57, 92, 93
SIGINT. *See* Signals Intelligence (SIGINT)
Signals Intelligence (SIGINT), 10, 11, 12
source credibility, 22-23, 24, 25, 26, 27, 67,
   68
staffing plan (for Terrorism Forecasting System), 8, 51-57, 93
Strategic/Countrywide Indicator, 10, 11,12,
   19, 37, 39, 54, 55, 83
structured analytical technique, 2-3, 7, 8, 9,
   28, 47, 51, 62, 81, 93. *See also* systematic process
SWO. *See* Senior Warning Officer
systematic process, 2-3, 5, 7, 8, 42, 51, 63,
   85, 93, 94. *See also* structured analytical
   technique

"t," 30, 31,32, 33, 53, 93
"T," 30, 31, 32-33, 53, 77, 93
Tactical/Target Specific Indicator, 10, 12,

About the Author

Captain Sundri K. Khalsa has been a military intelligence officer in the United States Air Force since 1996 and developed this terrorism forecasting system while: 1) serving as the unit chief of a Counterintelligence/Counter-terrorism Analysis Cell in Riyadh, Saudi Arabia (August 2000-August 2001), 2) refining the system under academic scrutiny in a master's thesis at the Defense Intelligence Agency (DIA) Joint Military Intelligence College (August 2001-August 2002), and 3) improving the methodology's ability to incorporate law enforcement information when FBI and CIA officials invited her to implement the methodology at FBI Headquarters in September 2002.

She holds a B.A. in biochemistry from the University of Virginia, which gave her a foundation and appreciation for structured and scientific analytical techniques, and an M.S. in strategic intelligence from the Joint Military Intelligence College, known as "the Harvard of the intelligence field," where she graduated number 1 in her class of 115 civilian and military intelligence professionals.

Since entering the Air Force in 1996, she has served at the 315th Intelligence Training Squadron at Goodfellow Air Force Base in Texas; the 18th Wing Intelligence Flight at Kadena Air Base in Okinawa, Japan; U.S. Air Forces Europe Headquarters at Ramstein Air Base in Germany; the Air Force Office of Special Investigations 24th Expeditionary Field Investigations Squadron in Riyadh, Saudi Arabia; the Joint Military Intelligence College at the Defense Intelligence Agency in Washington, D.C.; the FBI Counterterrorism Division Threat Monitoring Unit in Washington, D.C.; Joint Interagency Task Force West in Alameda, California; the U.S. Embassy in Manila, Philippines; and Joint Interagency Coordination Group for Combating Terrorism at Camp Smith in Honolulu, Hawaii.